The Faithful Transcriber

Satsvarūpa dāsa Goswami

Collected Works of Satsvarūpa dāsa Goswami:

1996 Śrīla Prabhupāda Centennial Year Writings, Volume 6

The Faithful Transcriber

Satsvarūpa dāsa Goswami

Second Edition, 2024

This edition of Satsvarūpa dāsa Goswami's 1996 timed book, *The Faithful Transcriber*, is published as part of a legacy project to restore Satsvarūpa Mahārāja's writings to 'in print' status and make them globally available for current and future readers.

GN Press, Inc., gratefully acknowledges the BBTI for the use within this book of verses and purports from Śrīla Prabhupāda's books.

Books in this series:
1. May Apples
2. Basic Sketchbook
3. Upstate: Room to Write
4. June Bug
5. Geaglum Free Write Diary
6. Dublin Pieces
7. The Faithful Transcriber
8. Wicklow Writing Sessions
9. Writing Sessions at Manu's House
10. My Purpose at Isola di Albarella

GN Press, Inc.

Oxford | New Delhi | Perth

Collected Works of Satsvarūpa dāsa Goswami

1996 Śrīla Prabhupāda
Centennial Year Writings, Volume 7

The Faithful Transcriber

June 28–July 13, 1996

Satsvarūpa dāsa Goswami

GN Press, Inc.
Oxford | New Delhi | Perth

June 28, 1996

Dún Laoghaire Harbor (pronounced by Madhu as "Dun Leery"). We are in queue, waiting for the Stena Line last ferry to Holyhead, Wales. So, I'll start my July book and warm up to it.

⁂ ⁂ ⁂

Onboard. We can't stay in our van so join sojourners in the upstairs regions. So far at least it's not piped music but that may start. All one family? Children and moms and guys and grannies and people in charge. I don't really like to overhear them.

I am the faithful transcriber but I've offered myself the chance to tell "lies" too. To get under the surface of mere reporting, untruths or fictions, allowing fancies, may help.

The green zorch game, the Incredible Something, a fun-house you can enter, and a spacious tax-free, a duty-free shop. A McDonald's, alcoholic drinks served too.

Read yesterday Māyā Angelou's memoir about racial prejudice against African-Americans. Eudora Welty said, "Mine is a sheltered life." Then she said something daring about inner life.

I have a *Cc.* with me but I think I'll grow sleepy with anything I do. Missed my usual rest … Hare Kṛṣṇa.

This is the month beginning and I'm searching for what it is I'll write on in a way to make it vital.

He slept and didn't go down to Davy Jones'
locker. The video games when
you turn them on, make spurts of

music, weird sounds—and we are right near a batch of them. Now "Irish Sea … forty knots, ninety-nine minutes, but you'll have plenty of time to use all our facilities." Nonsense and noise. How can you write a thoughtful piece in this place? Lie down on the floor with your arms for a pillow?

So, a porpoise didn't leap out. "Ain't She Sweet?" —just a snatch from it from the video game. Then that gong, gong, gong lunacy sound. It's pretty bad. I don't want to take it out on you, dear reader, dear notepad, but writing sometimes helps.

Voice from the video game: "Hold it, hold it."

⁂ ⁂ ⁂

The boat entertainment is bombarding us and there is no escape. Maybe next time we'll stay illegally in our van—with risk you could drown if there's an emergency. Traveling in public this way is tough on the monk's sensibility.

We are in a small seating section but each section has its own video and loud sound for all—no choice. First, they showed a Hollywood film, "Alexander's Ragtime Band," circa 1920s or early 1930s. That was sentimentally amusing and I was mostly able to keep my eyes down and concentrate on *japa*, counter beads and *japa* beads. But other things were more disconcerting. One was a commercial for a video, *Predators*, which had close-up footage of animals attacking and devouring each other. The lion running, filmed in slow motion, catches up to the buffalo, pouncing, tearing his flesh. "Would you like a crocodile in your living room? Only the brave would film it."

Now, now. Hare Kṛṣṇa. What is it you will write and do? Your theme of life is to function as a devotee in the Kṛṣṇa consciousness movement. Kṛṣṇa is the goal. When the goal is assigned, then the path is slowly but progressively traversed.

Now, a "serious" cartoon of Dr. Jekyll and Mr. Hyde—a story to enthrall people, good and evil. (But I don't have time to write a story and don't want to.)

Faithful transcriber of what actually happens says, "I'm on the Stena Ferry, annoyed and now captured by the film, now Dr. Jekyll." So, I … I will be free of it eventually and these harmless images …

Wait. Dr. Jekyll, don't make your will out giving everything to Mr. Hyde. You should stand up for the good in you.

Kṛṣṇa, Kṛṣṇa, Kṛṣṇa. It will look good later. When we're out of the grips of "doing time" on the ferry, we'll be in our natural environ in the van, but have five hours of driving in Britain to reach the devotees' house. The theme of this book is yet to be found, but I want to find it …

⁂ ⁂ ⁂

Speeding in the van, I'm in the back, faithful transcriber. I'm going to keep repeating that to explore it. The bunk is a bit too short, the place to sit is too curvy for the spine. Those are the facts.

There is no point I see right now in making something up, even briefly. Say, "I got an idea to write from seeing Doctor Jekyll and Mr. Hyde." Did I? I ate four carob sweets. I lusted. I eulogized. I attained *kṛṣṇa-prema*, was sincere in my stay in London, spoke to disciples and realized I was a guru of sorts and willing to take it up. They say *ṛtvik* guru is big in England, and also a community has formed in South Wales, breaking away from their ISKCON guru.

The Manor is different. The manner—expect Satsvarūpa to shed some light? He at least is still with us all these years.

Yes, I want to write something more than this, but little fabrications don't seem sufficient. We will see. We will see.

Kṛṣṇa blew His Pāñcajanya conch and Arjuna blew his Devadatta—that picture is before me on the cover of *Message of Godhead*. M. is now able to roar forward with his massive American Ford engine and that is the good result of all the hassles we've gone through.

Natalie Goldberg techniques hold you in good stead? Will you write what the hand wills? Here we are in the back of the van, writing for the first time. Fixodent. *Kṛṣṇa Book*. My message is His message—don't kill cows, our scriptures are the best.

It's just the best band what am
my honey lamb.

I feel I want to tell M. the plot of "Alexander's Ragtime

Band"—what I saw of it and the harmless amusement of it as the guy sang, "In your Easter bonnet" on stage at Carnegie Hall. Not a black face appeared in the film, but that is where the music comes from. Pretended otherwise in the 1930s as if white folks created the music and Alexander just waves his white baton at the orchestra as they play "Swing music." A woman in a long gown came on stage and sang, "We're having a heat wave." I looked down during that one—even the 1930s can be torrid in its way, and Doctor Jekyll…Mr. Hyde committing murders on London Bridge. That film was still running when our boat docked in Holyhead.

Slowly it comes out, the tale I have to tell. May my reader be patient with me. I'll find a way.

Faster he goes from Wales to London and we hope we don't crash. He plans to double park on the street of row houses in London, offload me and boxes in Guru-daskṣiṇā's house and then he'll drive off to visit his mother. I'll be with him all day Saturday at Bhaktivedanta Manor and back to Guru-daskṣiṇā's.

We're having' a heatwave,
a tropical heatwave
the temperature's rising
isn't it surprising'
she certainly can can-can

Why should someone desert their ISKCON guru? I'm a good time guy, may not be pure, but what the heck? Whaddaya expect when you get bombarded as you travel … a thousand shocks.

Heading in. Hard rain. M. says this van handles much better than the other. I told him defects of writing in the back. Some can be adjusted.

Didn't tell him what?

A soul wants to free-write and find the way to Kṛṣṇa.

If your reading of Kṛṣṇa's scriptures doesn't provoke taste, then what good is merely following the rules? At least try reading and hearing. You're not going to make it by riding around in your van—you won't make it back to Godhead.

Come on and hear
come on and hear
Śrīmad-Bhāgavatam is here.

Author watching 'Dr. Jekyl + Mr Hyde'

Forty-five miles outside London. Rain has stopped. Rolling along.

I'll hear something and talk tomorrow. Say, "We have the best scriptures, but what good does that do you if you don't hear them (*nityaṁ bhāgavata-sevayā*) and develop love of

Kṛṣṇa? Just to say, "we are better" doesn't make you better. Better includes qualities of humility, *tṛṇād api*, and eagerness to chant and hear, and compassion to hear Kṛṣṇa consciousness, and faith in those topmost scriptures. So, this I hope to remember to say.

⁂ ⁂ ⁂

There is no better way. (Like this, as he races the engine, I can race a little to find those words of periphery of consciousness and write them down.)

gopīs—perspective
gopas—languish
pipes—neckties – Longfellow
Armitige, Armitige

scripture—Dead Sea pots, clay, cave, bluff, who really knows. Can you be true and call the Swami? —I don't mean sentimental self-serving, "Oh, I was there in the beginning, 1966,"—but something elemental and real.

rail—derail
hope—condemned
life—death

Write your own way. Rattle and race to London, Honey chile.

The scripture is the king of education, the most secret of secrets.

He said we will get there before 2:00 P.M. My program is to smile, say pleasantries and head for the bathroom to shower and then set Śrīla Prabhupāda up on the altar and receive *prasādam*. Madhu's program is to run around trying to fix a seat in the van or give the van to a mechanic to attach a gas tank underneath.

Brāhmaṇas—brāhmaṇa underwear, brahmin spaghetti, loose ends. Park square, get off. Fat man, looped thread.

Kṛṣṇa consciousness.

Oh, I could write a sonnet
about your Easter bonnet

That was a hilarious moment in "Alexander's Ragtime Band," when the corny guy sang that on the stage at Carnegie Hall. The thin plot of the movie, I couldn't quite grasp because I wasn't watching it. But while Alexander was having his grand triumph at the Carnegie Hall concert, his girl was wandering around nearby the city. Maybe she was in amnesia. At the very last number Alexander played, he turned to the audience and said he was playing this for a very special person. As he began to play, his girl, who was sitting in a taxi outside, began to cry. I looked down. The next moment I looked up again and there she was on stage, belting out the vocal to "Alexander's Ragtime Band." He was waving his hand, facing the orchestra and she was facing the audience and they lived happily ever after, reunited.

6:00 P.M.

Arrived okay at Guru-daskṣiṇā's house. Greeted there by affectionate devotees. Faithful transcriber doesn't mean you have to say everything. Not possible anyway. Select on what basis? To show yourself a genial guru? I asked what each one doing. Sat in an easy chair. I heard they had a typewriter for me, but it hasn't manifested yet. Aromatherapy: candle under porcelain cup, with a little water and some oils. Does it do anything? Sorry to hear that in G.D.'s opinion British are prejudiced against devotees. He told how it's better in

Australia, and that is due to Food for Life and other strategies whereby devotees are seen as people who are giving rather than taking.

I'm in the room on the third floor where I was last year before going to India to the health clinic.

Śrīla Prabhupāda didn't get his bath today. But we ate plenty.

Gopas—tomahawks, peripherals, those turbans and paintings of them. No, I can't leap. Can't leapfrog. Film ferry behind me now, like a ship's wake. This body, when standing in poor posture, has a protruding belly and terrible slouch. Stand straight like a military man. Throw back your shoulders.

I asked G.D. for an update on Mad Cow disease. He didn't know. I asked him about ISKCON controversies as they occurring in the Manor. He didn't know much. Says he stays out of that sort of thing, but he can direct me tomorrow to someone who knows. "No, thanks," I said.

The swift river. London to me is the shelter of this room and then tomorrow, the shelter of Śrīla Prabhupāda's temple, Bhaktivedanta Manor, where I receive the honor to read *Cc.*

"You get up at midnight?" We'll see. Write your memoirs. I remember a pinch in the butt. I recall Alexander Rag. I am filled with unholy allusions. But now my reputation is not: "the skinny guy in black sweater and black pants and dirty, low cut tennis shoes? The sex-frustrated poet?" No, my rep is that humble, bewildered *sannyāsī*, that going-out flame.

Aromatherapy, the wildlife—lion attacked the buffalo. You don't want more of that. Drive to the Manor and see the statues. That's what the pious do.

⁂ ⁂ ⁂

The Faithful Transcriber

Tell us tomorrow
what a pious devotee thinks.
How he's not envious
and holds the line.

June 29, 1996

They can take the flesh, they can take the horn, the hide, the hoof. They can take the cow after it dies a natural death. The *muci* comes and takes the cow away. So, let her live and the *muci* class will come when the cow is dead and from that cow hide, they will make shoes …

But no slaughter house.

The milk is nothing but cow's blood transformed. Take her milk but let her live.

You ask yourself how dedicated you are to saving Mother Cow. It is one of the items of the Kṛṣṇa consciousness movement. People don't care about it. Witness in the Mad Cow disease when they saw they had to kill cows. No one was concerned. Śrīla Prabhupāda didn't live with cows as a cowherd man but he lived with them in Vṛndāvana. Every Indian knows the cow is one of your mothers. You drink her milk.

So, repeat these things and be confident. You first always admit your littleness and failures, your contrariness. And then go further beyond it. I too care. That means feel pain over infamy. Anger and action. But what action can you take in Kali-yuga? It seems to be a hopeless cause, like celibacy or the vegetarian movement. It doesn't matter. Preach and be true. Advise people to chant Hare Kṛṣṇa and hear about Kṛṣṇa consciousness, to read Śrīla Prabhupāda's books and the rest may come automatically. Hare Kṛṣṇa Hare Kṛṣṇa, Kṛṣṇa Kṛṣṇa Hare Hare.

You may take her flesh, her hoof and horn after she dies a natural death. But no. They can't wait.

⁘ ⁘ ⁘

They can't wait. I am up at twelve because I have promised. I wanted to come to the page and write before some inner organ makes a pain and one has to rush to the hospital and stop writing. Write and say, "Okay, I did."

We did not milk the *sadhu*
for all we could and then

reject him. I did not. It is more complicated than that. They served and worshipped him sincerely and were forced to stop. When forced they also realized it is better that we worship our Śrīla Prabhupāda and the exact emphasis he gives in Kṛṣṇa consciousness.

After Śrīla Prabhupāda there is now a multiplicity of leaders and followers and camps. Splits. No splits if you are sincere, he said. Splits have occurred, like it or not.

⁂ ⁂ ⁂

Artist sketching

Tot, watchya got? I got millions of tricks and rivets. I couldn't sleep and went out on the roof. I met a ghost, a wrench, a wraith of London. He spoke of all evils and a bad man held up a big monkey wrench to hit me and I crawled back into the skylight, into my dreams. And what were they? I put them aside, couldn't take them seriously enough to retain them.

And was there a typewriter brought overnight by Sooty Santa?

No, nothing of the sort. Woke and by the strength of my thumb I am writing. Neck bent down and lamplight.

Are you ashamed to write of yourself? No, why should I be?

The clock ticks. While the clock ticks I write. Drive, he said, a little after four through dark and wet streets to the Manor, mock Georgian slats against cement outer walls, that friendly-to-me building because we saw His Divine Grace here.

Men chanting Hare Kṛṣṇa

Oh, come, you don't love him so much. You are affected by the rosy "all's well" sentimentality of that 1930s film you saw yesterday.

No, I ain't. I ain't. You blimey … I am truly a *śiṣya* and that's the way it is. But I do appreciate your warning, Śrī Gremlin, not to portray myself as a saint, as a faultless one. To London I also came in wrong moods too.

Please bless us, please let us be pure.

And write a little longer what the master says. From your tongue inspired.

The sirens go on.

Gathering in criminals from the streets. Now, instead of one Mr. Hyde there are millions. Who knows the evil?

Śrīla Prabhupāda

⁘ ⁘ ⁘

I've seen this during my times. I've drawn the fruit many times. I've ridden to the Manor many times. I've faked it many times. Outlived, lived through, stood in there on the same legs and subdued my flesh and head …

And that's just this one lifetime, American Joe.

Then? They die one by one or sometimes more than that.

Kṛṣṇa, Kṛṣṇa. Horrid deaths.

Please be kind, please be intelligent. He speaks with *buddhi-yoga* given by the Lord. He serves in a checkered career.

⁂ ⁂ ⁂

Did you really go on the roof in your skivvies, your nightgown, and see Lewis Carrol and Charles Dickens and ghosts of cities? No rats present, I hope.

No, I stayed snug a few hours, and now I'm here splayed and failing.

Recall a word when you were not British, recall a time when your mom loved you and you clung to her arm, her ample, fleshy arm and said, "Mom, I want your love, I am you little angel one." "I am Wimpy," the waitress said, "because I ate so many burgers." Gosh, you think that's cute?

What did we know?

We were so ignorant. Take compassion on them by teaching Kṛṣṇa consciousness. That's what the pen is for.

Mommy, if you pray to God …

I am doing that. We know Him as Kṛṣṇa and you worship His son (one of many) as Jesus Christ.

Oh, please take it right, take it rightly. God the Father is pleased with you. I didn't like the Sunday school version as a life of Christ.

Now finish. I close out this one. Forgive. Forgive. Go

forward. The dirty river, the Thames, the river Lethe, St. Lawrence, mixed with blood and filth. Mixed with purpose and porpoise and fear. We'll get there, death day, of course. And as for remembering and loving Lord Kṛṣṇa, He is present in our lives and it's a fact and your Swami confirms.

⁂ ⁂ ⁂

10:40 A.M.

You're going to have write here sometimes rushed, without feeling completely into it if you want to write at all this month. The morning program at the Manor went well, but my head got weak. They let me go to the *sannyāsī* room after *maṅgala-ārati.* I lay my head on the pillow for fifteen minutes and overcame the first weakness. But then it came again.

So, when I was sitting on the *vyāsāsana* and the room full of devotees was bowing down during the recitation of *prema dvani* by me, I gulped down my headache pill. It carried me through and I am still going strong. But I have two appointments for the afternoon. I'm going to visit the old original Śyāmasundara dasa at 4:00 P.M. I told them I could spare him half an hour. Then I'll come back to this house and meet with my disciples. If my head is weak, I'll take another pill. This is called coping with allopathic medicine. I hope it doesn't build up. I won't let it. And one hopes that it does not have side effects. But it is better than canceling a whole day at the first waves of head weakness. That's how I felt about it this morning. There I was, with rows and rows of devotees sitting before me. Śacīnandana said that more devotees came than usual on a Saturday morning. So, I was going to lecture to them with pain, and therefore not be able to exert myself on the vital topics (cow killing and descriptions of the *yavanas* in *Cc.*)? No, I decided, go ahead, your doctor said it is not excessive.

I wanted to report that to you, dear diary, dear Manu.

⁂ ⁂ ⁂

You mean there is one person to whom you would like to address this whole book? How about to your Doctor Alexander? Or how about to Poof, the Toof? A fictional mentor or shoulder to cry on? How about a New Age writing teacher or to Robert Bly, and you try to preach to him? No, please be serious and don't josh around.

But this going to be a joshing month in writing. It's one of our main themes. We feel we can be more serious by joshing sometimes. I think you've heard that enough from me. As for addressing someone, you can do it sometimes. Don't set up binding rules that "this shall always be the way we do this from now on."

So, I was saying it was a good morning. Next week they have their victory celebration, which is actually their Ratha-yātrā. They are celebrating the awarding of permission to build the access road to the Manor. I congratulated them on this. I spoke my speech. I mouthed my piece. I showed up in the old flesh. I walked out during the *kīrtaning* and got some fresh air. Saw the ducks and the black-necked geese on the lawn. The tall pole with the flag of Hanumān on top, a symbol of the fight to keep the Manor open. Noticed mostly young devotees and very few Prabhupāda disciples, typical of most ISKCON temples. What does it mean? Oh, Sats, you did okay and didn't eat too much for breakfast. Refused the pancakes and took just mango slices and creamed almond nuts and hot apples. This is one busy day and then tomorrow travel, travel in the van. Hare Kṛṣṇa Hare Kṛṣṇa, Kṛṣṇa Kṛṣṇa Hare Hare.

⁂ ⁂ ⁂

I lay down for a few minutes on my back before lunch. I heard a heavy thump, thump, thump. I thought maybe it was an electric bass, music maybe coming from a car in the street or an apartment. At the same time, I relaxed further into the soft bed. Then the thump, thump reminded me of a bass drum like you'd hear in a marching band, live, not recorded. I thought of such bands and how you'd hear them a block away when you are waiting for a parade. Then I thought of marching bands and how they played peppy tunes like, "Poppa loves Tango, Momma loves Tango." Perhaps that's not the name of the song. Was it, "Momma loves mumbo," or Momma loves something? Then I hummed a tune to myself. Then my train of thought went to Pearl Berly and that pop song of hers, "It takes two to tango." I remember the words: "It takes two to tango, two to tango, two to really do...let's do the tango, do the dance of love." I thought how Pearl Berly really conveyed lust in her singing. She was not, I think, an esteemed jazz singer or Blues singer. Taken advantage of by the whites and their idea of a black singer, lusty and comical.

I wanted to record these thoughts in the chain they occurred. Manu dasa said that my books seem to be in part an attempt to give evidence that I'm not a pure devotee. I'm chipping down any pretense or false image. So, there it is folks. That's what I thought of when I rested and relaxed. And it is not so much due to a lusty or evil intention on my part, but my background. Memories. It is also the environment—if you lie down drowsily and start hearing Rādhe-Śyāma, Rādhe-Śyāma, maybe the train of thought goes somewhere better.

⁂ ⁂ ⁂

3:10 P.M.

Write something nice. Vāsudeva Datta prayed that all living beings be liberated from their sins and made eligible for love of God. He was willing to take all sins upon himself so that others could be saved. He was universal love personified. This is the spirit of a great Vaiṣṇava. Lord Caitanya said to Vāsudeva Datta, "Because you desire the release of all conditioned souls, it will be done, because My will is to satisfy My devotees." He said Vāsudeva Datta was the incarnation of Prahlāda.

Care for others. Sacrifice for them in some way. Go see an old devotee who asks you to do so. Then meet with those who have taken initiation from you. Remind them of the goal of life and how to attain it. The goal is not eating-mating-sleeping-defending. Get free of this world.

June 30, 1996

There are innumerable universes, like seeds in a mustard pot. Or like the fruits of an *uḍumbara* tree. If one is lost, it does not constitute a loss for Kṛṣṇa. So, if by the desire of a great devotee like Vāsudeva Datta, all the souls are delivered to Kṛṣṇa from a universe, it can be done. Reading this just now, I think of those souls who pray to God for deliverance of others. I'm acquainted with some of the saints who did it by appealing to Jesus Christ. But it takes sacrifice and we are not willing to pay that price. Similarly, we are unwilling to deliver even our own self. We don't to want to enter the feeling of helplessness of the child calling for their mother.

⁘ ⁘ ⁘

I have not accepted wholeheartedly yet that this book is about writing the book. I will faithfully transcribe events and then do something else, like indulge in memories—word, place, and so on. This repertoire is all I have so far and so I will go with it. I seem to be seeking a repertoire, tour de force, if possible, and unity of chapters.

Met with Śyāmasundara and Dhanañjaya yesterday. It was enlivening to sit with them and talk of old days with Prabhupāda. Śyāmasundara is back to his former preaching of being with George Harrison in an intimate way. They sat with him the other night while he played the guitar and he (Śyāmasundara) and Mukunda Mahārāja made up Kṛṣṇa conscious lyrics which they are trying to inject in George's latest albums. Śyāmasundara said George has again become very popular and rich through a revival of Beatles music. I was happy to hear that, then told Śyāmasundara that I remember how he was the first one to write creatively, with a stream of consciousness, when he was Śrīla Prabhupāda's secretary. I encouraged him to do it again. Dhanañjaya said he estimated that one third of Prabhupāda's recorded lectures and talks have been lost over the years. Especially from the early years. Śyāmasundara said that maybe he would seek to find them. I thought later, let me go on listening to whatever lectures of Prabhupāda we do have.

⁂ ⁂ ⁂

It is not wrong to track down my thoughts and feelings in my own book. It's basic integrity to do so. One memoirist, Patricia Hampl, says people accuse memoirists (the same could be said of diarists) of being self-centered, narcissistic. But she doesn't buy that theory. She says when you contact your own memories (and feelings) you contact the world. The "I" in the memoir is not the center of everything but the protagonist in the whole tragedy of human existence. In Kṛṣṇa conscious terms the "I" becomes self-realized, servant of God, a preacher and disciple of the pure devotee. Thus, we hear of Kṛṣṇa, Kṛṣṇa consciousness and all souls in an impersonal way. The big topics can be discussed among friends.

Therefore, keep mining. There is gold in Madagascar, thinks Śyāmasundara, and he will go on mining for one more year to make enough so he can write memoirs of Prabhupāda and his years with him. Time is short, I feel it. I have tolerable health but it can be taken away. I must tell this story month by month. It doesn't matter to the universe whether I tell these stories, perhaps, but it matters to me. And it helps some people. It is my way of serving.

To devotees last night I read that Lord Caitanya told three different persons to serve Kṛṣṇa in three different ways. Mukunda and his two sons, Raghunātha and Narahari. Lord Caitanya told Mukunda to be a *gṛhastha* businessman (physician) and to serve Kṛṣṇa in that way. Narahari should preach and live with the devotees, and Raghunandana should do Deity worship. We serve in any capacity but serve sincerely. A *brahmacārī* from New York said, "But I thought Prabhupāda said book distribution is the most important service."

I paused and said, "Yes, Prabhupāda said that but he also said other services were more important." Prabhupāda told me when I was in Dallas that I was doing the most important service in *gurukula*. I referred to the 1975 letter where Prabhupāda told me that it was childish for the devotees to fight among themselves and say that book distributors only could become *gopis*. He said pleasing Kṛṣṇa was not confined to a particular department or *asrama* but based on sincerity. He also said that of the nine principles of *bhakti*, *kīrtana* and *śravaṇaṁ* are most important. Again, I could have said more but I didn't. I could have said that book distributors are on the frontlines and we should give them the most respect. I could have said that all forms of preaching are important. Preaching is the essence. Another leader may have said, "Yes, book distributors are the most pleasing of all." I prefer to think that we can all please Prabhupāda in our individual ways, according to our sincerity. Lord Caitanya emphasized the quality of one's chanting and the extent to which one realizes the holy name is Kṛṣṇa and his spreading of the chanting. I didn't get all that out last night. I have more chances to do it in the coming weeks, the meeting at Rādhā-deśa. The preacher gets warmed up to his topic and the transcriber will follow him. Record today (I hope) how we easily entered the European continent with our van with Pennsylvania license plates.

⁂ ⁂ ⁂

Le Shuttle—the first time for us. Leave behind old thoughts in England. I told Madhu about George Harrison and all that. A man my age shouldn't be interested in … Another thing is …

This material world has enough gadgets and problems to keep you occupied and forgetful of Kṛṣṇa.

Travel news: I decided to try to drive all the way to Rādhā-deśa in one day. Our original plan was to stay overnight on the road. I do have a bit of a headache but if you take a pill… Staying on the road doesn't make it easier. We didn't talk it out thoroughly. Strain, strain, you take it a little. Toilet, Le Shuttle, "Have you tried Club Class?" What formalities at the border? It costs £149 round trip. We are a high vehicle. Good-bye.

Mahārāja, are you still getting headaches?

Yes.

I heard you are taking allopathic medicine.

Yes, it doesn't stop the headaches, but the symptoms. I got a headache yesterday, just before the lecture.

Oh!

Yes, I didn't take any pills for ten years but had to cancel so many engagements and was becoming more and more reclusive. I'm not taking any narcotics.

Then that conversation was cut-off. It was me and Guru-dakṣiṇā and his wife and sister-in-law. But M. came in and said we were ready to go. I went to use their bathroom. If

I had had time, I would have talked some more about it. "Please keep it a secret." No, you can't say that. But you might say, "If the pill-taking escalates, I'll have to see. This is what happened before." I found people interested in my condition. Talk with them about it. No time. Out the door.

Driving, drowsing to the Channel tunnel. A Band-aid on the thumb and one on the longest finger of my right hand so I don't rip skin while chanting *japa*. I think I'm getting a headache. My neck and back are also stiff. It's good to tell *you* these things.

If I could find out how *you* are, to whom I am speaking, that might help. Or perhaps better leave it as it is, dear reader, or confidential self, as in Anne Frank's "Dear Kitty" to whom she wrote her diary.

⁘ ⁘ ⁘

Racing in France. Back of the van not comfortable yet. Will it ever be? Cramped. Stretch a leg. Now, tell us. My lungs are a bit filled with phlegm.

> You report your body pains
> and mental shifts as if they

were weather changes of importance to the nation. Mind rides on a rail-like Le Shuttle under the Channel. A car within a railroad car.

Haribol. Clean out your dentures, put in new adhesive and eat another meal.

You are determined to expose your follies and to become serious by reciting scripture. Fool recites. Told last night what Lord Caitanya told Satyarāja Khan regarding the importance of chanting and serving Vaiṣṇavas.

Visiting sannyāsī and driver

Hey, man, they all want to hear some nectar and instruction from Vaiṣṇava *smṛti*, what Prabhupāda gives—so, give it to them. That's your guruship.

Raccoon. Rabbit. Wildlife on the highway. A wigwam descends. The loony things depicted on billboards. One shows a man jamming a small cactus plant into his mouth. In the name of faithful transcriber, don't feel obliged to tell all nonsense.

Hrdy, heart. Heartburn.

The trail. The list of things you'll do at Rādhā-deśa. You can always tell us that and then it's just the diary of a son on the camping trip, a religious minister in his duties, day after day. They're giving us someone's summer home to use. So, Madhu can work on the van and I'll be more comfortable. Prepare for classes and do this writing and some unmotivated reading.

⁂ ⁂ ⁂

Dangle I do from
Swami
like a spider dangles down,
connected by the thread.

Sigh and breathe and say okay. M. says we will stop and have lunch.

SDG gesturing while sitting

Drawing at 80 mph.

Stopped for lunch. Bear witness. What you see of the universe. And you can claim it as a disciple. No dispute with others regarding what they may see, but this is what you see.

At Rādhā-deśa I'll be on good behavior. Public ministry. Yet when I play the tape excerpt of Śrīla Prabhupāda and speak something, I hope it will be true, not lies. You do like it. And you do wish to get them interested in this. Appreciate what our master is saying. This is a real observance of the Centennial.

Public/private. This writing is more than the private side of life. It includes the foibles and the facts of the body. Body imperfect. Self still covered and he heads to his death. Don't make a myth of the perfect spiritual master who sees his (her) *mañjarī* service.

3:10 P.M.

Last hour before we reach Rādhā-deśa. You don't feel so great but you'll be relieved to get to the destination. Soon the mail will arrive there and I feel it may threaten this writing project, squeeze it to a small part of my life. Resist that. One needs time and space to explore these premises, not lose the thread.

Golden thread
Blake

Kṛṣṇa, Kṛṣṇa, Sārvabhauma invited Lord Caitanya to dinner and Amogha criticized the Lord. I turn to the illustration Amogha, a tiny figure running away, Sārva with the stick. His wife beating her chest, "Let my daughter become a widow!" Lord Caitanya laughing and saying, "Amogha didn't do anything wrong." I was thinking to show it to M. to justify eating a lot. No need, a *sannyāsī* shouldn't overeat.

Don't blaspheme a devotee. Go away from that place or you'll fall down.

Don't berate.

Raindrops on the window. Powerful engine. Dark sky. If we arrive at 4:00 P.M., Hṛdaya Caitanya may be outside waiting for us.

Tell him, “Oh, I’m tired from the road.” Thousands of overhead lamps on the highway. Turn off the main highway. Do you need another pill? Luxembourg. Arlon. Marche. Arrows, bridges, rails, scenes of battles in world wars, green now over graves.

What is it called? Petit something? We are not there yet. I need a lift.

Visiting sannyāsī and driver, front view

July 1, 1996

Received a letter from Trivikrāma Swami asking me to visit him in Poland. He says, "Have been reading some of your books … I am happy and proud that you have succeeded in your attempt to be true to your own nature and, at the same time, make such a substantial contribution to Śrīla Prabhupāda's movement." Save that one. I said to Madhu that if we were to go to Poland, the only reason would be just for the sake of friendship. He said if that's the reason, it would be worth it.

Gosh, all night M. does this very loud clearing of his throat. We are staying in a house they gave us, but it is like staying in one room. So, I just wrote him a note saying he'll have to sleep in the van, and he can use my bed.

Clenched fist. Whoever said that whatever you write can be called a book? Preposterous.

Preposterous to you, mister, not to us. We work at it hard and scratch our pen. Save dreams but now they have gone over the waterfall and I couldn't save them.

True to your nature, you must be. Saw a newsletter from a "social convention" on how to improve ISKCON's *varnas* and *asramas*. One question raised was why more *gṛhasthas* are not on the GBC. A *sannyāsī* replied that the GBC *sannyāsīs* are fed up with so much management and they would all like to go to "that farm in British Columbia or somewhere." He says they want to preach more— "We are going in that direction."

You look for a sign in the weather that will prove you right, give you permission. But you can't wait. Right now, the desk lamp creates a big shadow of my writing fist but I can't wait to fix it. See?

Did you drive long? Yes. Kids waiting here to give us little bunches of wildflowers. They are waiting an hour for us because we didn't know there was an hour change from England to Europe. Oh, the train tunnel is a very good line, you can eat your breakfast and in a total of thirty-five minutes you're on the other side. Better than the ferry. I don't know how I'll get so deep but it's possible.

Kṛṣṇa, Kṛṣṇa, Kṛṣṇa. Tell people about Kṛṣṇa and how to improve their consciousness. It is definitely preaching to oneself. I have one day to get my seminar ready. You know this. I'm not telling you something new. Recording it to look at later. Come here and give four classes of playing his tapes in segments and then saying, "Here, I like this for a special reason. Now you please take it too if you can. Appreciate hearing the tapes of our spiritual master." Got basic excerpts, got music, and joy and jokes and teeth and head and ... But each is one alone.

I told you he gave me a book, *Hermits*. It's an ordinary run-through history of hermits in various cultures. A terrible example is given to represent India; I won't soil the page by mentioning it. But I'm looking at the other sections. They valued the individual over society. In ancient Greek culture, the highest value was to the well-thought-of in society, but Socrates created a sea change in that attitude. He lived in a city, but did not follow ordinary people's norms. Hermits are generally ascetics. I'll let you know more—tidbits from it.

Remember that dream of a few days ago; we were observing Śrīla Prabhupāda in his intimate relationship with one servant. Our relationship to him was awe and reverence, and avoiding neglect at all costs. But the servant was eating his own fruit and not serving Prabhupāda breakfast. Later, we saw Prabhupāda massaging the head of this servant. We found out that Śrīla Prabhupāda heard his servant didn't give the master breakfast because the servant didn't feel well. Prabhupāda therefore massaged him. They even expressed anger toward each other but it was in love. Trying to figure that one out, although I can't and don't want to take it cheaply—that you can be angry with your guru and neglect him and yet you love him. But it did seem to indicate something beyond official relationships.

Śrīla Prabhupāda, please accept me, we each as our heartbeat. Lord Caitanya instructed devotees in different ways. A disciple asked Śrīla Prabhupāda in Atlanta before a packed room, "How can we please you the most?" He replied, "By loving Kṛṣṇa."

By loving Kṛṣṇa, guru is pleased
the attempt to do it is the cowboy
wrestling down the wild bull
of his own mind.

Are you pleased? James Baldwin, in a story about a jazz musician, said he stood blowing his sax and the sound was (as if) crying out, "Do you love me? Do you love me?"

If you sit too long, you're going to get piles—like the bus drivers. You're joining to be a pile of an ant hill, like Hiraṇyakaśipu in *tapasya*, your fingernails will grow long (not mine) and your hair will be matted and knotted and finally you will see the Lord in your heart—maybe.

But if you chant Hare Kṛṣṇa and move about
you'll have a story to tell of
music flow and some things that
happened on the *bhakti* trail. We

went to one door to distribute a
book and a man came out with
a shotgun. He didn't want *any*
talk
but just said that we should get away.
So, we did.

How long can you go here? Can you click at the typewriter keys or will that be too loud? But it is a good variety of expression.

⁂ ⁂ ⁂

Kṛṣṇa, however, is permitted
and even call out to Him
Kṛṣṇa! Hare! O Rādhā and Kṛṣṇa

as a child calls out for his mother. That may also not be a refined angel's call, but it could be perfected and refined over centuries to become a monk's or nun's song, a *kīrtana* for entertaining and livening up dulled folks.

Man in motion

⁂ ⁂ ⁂

Give it a try. I can't be stopped by the fact that M. may wake up. He kept me up with throat clearing and now I keep him up by pen scratching and typewriting. Lord Caitanya ate at Sārvabhauma's and then went home. He was satisfied by the big meal. Does that mean you can imitate Him and take a plate of rice overflowing with ghee? No. So then what happened?

Sārva took Him home and then left and went back home. He and his wife discussed what to do over the fact that their son-in-law had offended the Lord.

⁘ ⁘ ⁘

The whole point is to write as much as possible. Express your thoughts and maybe you will hit something. You mean like a collective unconsciousness of the whole race? A stratum of truth speaking for all devotees? But they will have to be willing to accept it as flailing. You set yourself up as too much of an exception. Don't be a daredevil. And yet you should shoot for the white rhino. I spoke with the old Śyāmasundara and now I realized that he was the original daredevil, the one who tried big things for Prabhupāda. Prabhupāda approved of that spirit of his. He was the one who got the Manor through George and did many things like that. Big helium balloon over the city of Bombay, creating the Hare Kṛṣṇa festival. So, Śyāmasundara was telling us the real version according to himself, of why Prabhupāda went to Zurich. We never heard that before. He said that other devotees came to see Prabhupāda and they disapproved of speculating on the gold market. Śyāmasundara said that Prabhupāda told them, "Yes, you should not do it. It's not good for you. But Śyāmasundara can do it." That's dangerous. But maybe there's some scope for it. Someone can do things that others cannot … So, you say things like you want to write automatic writing and let the collective unconsciousness come through you. You have a license to write imperfectly, but do you want a batch of free-writers to come after you? I can't prevent that in any case.

At least I will try to set a better standard. I can't keep quiet just so that Madhu will sleep. Although one could set the example of just being a nice, quiet guy. There are different examples of what to do. Each of us has to put it on the line. No one is perfect.

7:05 A.M.

Do you need to prepare before a disciples' meeting? Yes, to some degree. But you also can go in there winging. You can pick out a *śāstra* to read or a topic. That you'll do elsewhere in notes. This is your premier book. This is your nook-rook. I am sorry and not sorry. You are getting performance oriented. If it gets too much so, then I will have to ditch this whole thing. I warn you. I feel the same way about the van. If it becomes too much of a trip of M. telling me what I can and can't do in there and how I have to live, then who needs it? Oh, come on, you are not so independent and self-sufficient as that. You get carried where someone wants to take you.

Some things
are best
renounced

Oh, yeah. We'll see.

At least in my own writing I am more self-sufficient. No one can tell me what to do here. Well, almost no one. Kṛṣṇa and guru direct me. But they also say to me, "Go ahead and do what you want. Make it a good flight of free-will and come winging back home to us. Your flight will be useful to others who will see the joy, freedom and faithfulness."

Stop worrying how it turns out, whether it's serious enough and so on.

⁂ ⁂ ⁂

It's cold here, I wish they had some heating system. I went out to chant around 2:00 A.M. and the sky was covered with clouds. The full moon peaked out like a gold coin only once in a while, and was covered again. Big snails in their shells. I stepped on one and cracked it by accident. I could have been more careful. I knew they were there. Near the cracked one, I removed the others from the path where I walked. Hare Kṛṣṇa. Kṛṣṇa, please forgive us our sloppy, giant's ways as we hope to not be squashed by demons and demigods in their play.

Hare Kṛṣṇa comes straight from Kṛṣṇaloka. By looking at *harināma* in the eye, you cannot yield the nectar. But hearing in your own way, no, it has to be done by invoking the mercy of the name on you. Only if the holy name wants to descend, does he or she do it. Drowsy. Now you could take another rest.

9:20 A.M.

Writing for me should be like chanting *japa*. You enter it as you would the extra rounds or the rounds before you reach sixteen. You have to do it. It is a prime way for reaching God. God is in His name. Chant, chant. Write, write. Kṛṣṇa wants you to do it. Writing is different because my words are not absolute. But my chanting also falls short in the absolute sense because my mind wanders and soul is covered. So, writing is good. Even if it always falls short. It is the record of me trying to go in.

I don't think it's so healthy for me to talk a lot about what I'm doing. For example, to sit around with literary friends, or to give interviews and advocate what I'm doing. I do enough writing about writing in the writing itself. It's a private world. It may be that I suffer from lack of discourse with competent persons. But I think that may be suffering in loneliness, and even that is a blessing. I don't think my writing needs to be criticized. What would I gain? I don't need teachers. I need better spiritual life. And I need to look into various books and writers who I think may help.

Madhu just showed me Śaunaka Ṛṣi's journal reporting the top-level interfaith meeting that took place in Wales. The Christian representatives were high-placed, open and respectful. They went deeply into dialogue with ISKCON's participants. I asked myself why don't I take part in that sort of thing. After all, I am open to hearing from such people. I guess the answer is this: this is another field which is not mine. I don't have a deep interest in it. And it is not something that you enter if you are lacking in interest. I don't want to boast that I'm better. But say here what you are. Simple. Committed to this search for self-expression through private writing. I do have respect for these dialogues and I'm glad ISKCON members are doing it. It overrules the fanatical side which only recognizes other religions to put them down. These dialogists inform us, make us truly humble. It's good. It is the kind of thing that is not just cosmetic work, but real work. However, it is not mine.

Exclude yourself if you will. But don't make out that you're the best. And don't feel self-pity when you're not included in such rewarding encounters. Don't make a story of yourself as the excluded Artist. It's just your way and that may also be subject to revision. You might take part in some things like that in the future. And if you did, it's not that you will speak as the most brilliant one present. You would make your own fair offering. In basketball I was never tall, and didn't have a good jump shot. Never made any teams. Same with baseball. I can make some teams in ISKCON, but I'm not an all-star. It would be absurd to withhold from all taking part because you wanted to preserve an image of being the best at everything. "I'm the best and I don't have to prove it by interacting." Better to take part sometimes and expose yourself as not the best. Show that you are willing to work with a team and come out of it, returning to your own person. And in your diary, also, you're not such an extremist like a Thoreau or a Kafka of ISKCON. Just a fellow who likes to write.

⁂ ⁂ ⁂

It's July 1st. I'm still waiting for this one to take off. Do you dare allow your imagination to fly? Well, that's it, Prabhu, I'm too conservative to do anything but recite *śāstra* and faithfully transcribe.

⁂ ⁂ ⁂

A ten-minute fight with a gremlin before lunch.

I remember the time I was outside this morning and chanting and looking up at the clouds over the moon, the way some nearby wisps blew quickly over the face of the moon. Right now, I think: is my writing effort entirely phony? You used to carry a very tightly wrapped umbrella and wear tight pants. Like that, is your writing an effectuation to look stylish?

No, not entirely. What about being a devotee and writer? One would say you couldn't make it in the material world of sex and money-making, so you copped out and became a devotee celibate cultist. Similarly, you wouldn't make it in the writing-publishing world, and so opted for this world where your brothers and your own movement (who are your disciples) publish your writings.

What else? You couldn't discipline yourself to write

stories, essay, and especially to rewrite, so you have opted for this loose form of free-writing, with no rewriting, just omitting the weakest parts.

And what else? No, you've said enough. I push at your face. I ignore you. Begin again.

I remember squeaks, people working against me. The scholars, the emotions, doing what you want. Alone at 125 Katan Avenue, trying to get high drinking, what was it? Cinnamon or some harmless thing, they said if you took enough of it, you'd get high. It didn't happen. You were saved from getting worse.

I remember I will tear this page up. I'm not getting anywhere. I don't know what is good and what is not good. Kṛṣṇa...You said you needed a fix, so go now and read *Caitanya-caritāmṛta*, it's what you need.

⁂ ⁂ ⁂

2:45 P.M.

Rain driving. Cold. They say it will be warm by Wednesday. Met with Śaunaka Ṛṣi and Hṛdaya Caitanya. Śaunaka said, "If you want to get your van out of trouble, you present your disciples to go there and say you are an important spiritual person. Let them do the work." That is a long story I haven't told here. It was a story that preceded this book (yes, this is a book that happens in July). It is the story of how we shipped our van to Ireland and the troubles to get it out of customs. That's told in that little book called *Dublin Pieces*, and in an even previous work called *Geaglum Free-write Diary*. Now, hear this one ... Śaunaka asked me, "Do you take suggestions for books to write?" I said, "Yes, but I not may use them." I also told them that when it is busy, as at this European convention, then my actual work becomes unbusy. I was coyly referring to writing. I said, “Writing takes place best when it appears that nothing is happening. When I am busy, I may write a diary and catch the energy in that way. But when it is quiet, I can go deeper and write on texts.” These things are not false and yet …

Whatever it was, after I took rest and woke (after lunch) I thought maybe what I’m doing is too splayed out and shouldn’t be continued. What? You mean we are back at that pre-lunch Gremlin fight?

I suppose we never left it. Just took a break from it. As the seminar bulletin reads, “Morning session, then break, then afternoon session.” So, I go on with my writing and doubt bouts.

It’s a diary scoop of events and sometimes something else that never perhaps happened.

July 2, 1996

During the night—two military dreams in which you failed to come up to the required bravery. Then a third dream of a book of photographs of a military reserve group. You and others looked through the book approvingly. You commented that the captions to the photos were "telling." They contained an understated criticism of war, yet an acceptance and even pride to have taken part in this experience of war games. A person who produced the book said, "At first I couldn't sell many copies until they put a photo of a soldier on the cover." It had looked like a dull book only for military reservists until they put the lively photo there.

What does it mean? The "military" life is required and I have to find the context in which I can serve? Maybe I can't fight physically but can produce a book from experiences as a reservist (unwilling reservist).

Preparing to rise from bed

Unwilling to rise at midnight. Mind saying you can't do it, too many preaching duties in the temple schedule. The little wars you need to endure—war to keep fighting for your kind of writing and believing in it, war against *māyā's* temptations against the wider *māyā* in the world which opposes ISKCON, war to endure the smallness of the routine that is life. War of *japa*.

Reaching for eyeglasses

⁂ ⁂ ⁂

Peaceful Belgium where jets pass low overhead. We talk of how to improve ISKCON. Everyone has a bit to play. Trying to contribute. Here is something I cooked, I sewed, I welded, I hoed, I rowed, I wrote, painted, worshipped, mothered, earned and gave this money—all for Kṛṣṇa. There was a dance and a song for Him. Hare Kṛṣṇa, the way and the goal. Can't get the desk lamp right, the head unstuck, the pen to flow just right, but in each case, I manage something. Śrīla Prabhupāda has his Dictaphone. Did he ever experience frustration or desire to make a purport better? He seemed to be humble, perfect. Never concocted, said what previous teachers said. No frustration of, "I think. In my opinion. Perhaps" when you say that you are not in knowledge. No frustration or false ego. Preach with devotion.

There was no return trip to Boston. That was a mistake. I

corrected the galley proofs. I reached for the stars. Rode as a galley slave. The Spanish translated prayer retreat as "prayer retirement." Oh, oh. These are not my duties—to make the whole history a clear memoir or an urgent poem. But do run on despite flowing nose and prose. Who told you this was okay? My own experience in *Shack Notes.*

Write fast and edit the best. I belong to this school. Write at midnight with your heart and palpitate. I, tightrope walker can't doubt or a fire walker. In outer space. Mumble, "One giant step for Mankind," —hoax that was but this is me actually here in Belgium, trying to find out who I is, where we is and how to be honest under the cover.

I've come here to give the seminar called, "Prabhupāda Appreciation," but it is not something I worry about or spend much time on. I have prepared the tape excerpts long in advance. Now, it's up to me to be "prepared" myself by listening to them. I listen to tapes other than the ones I will play in the class. Be prepared to be a devotee who is not phony, who can say something simple in appreciation, who can motivate others to do that. Be one who believes in the potency of the spiritual master's talking, who likes to listen to him. I prefer Śrīla Prabhupāda's lectures to his recorded conversations. During the conversations I remain tense, worrying whether the guest is being convinced. I keep thinking of the guest because he is the nondisciple of Prabhupāda. But in the lecture, I figure it's mostly his disciples, and somehow, I just place myself as one of them and hear what he has to say. But good things are certainly spoken in the conversations.

In one lecture in Geneva, he said to imagine that in your heart there is a diamond throne. Then imagine you are inviting the Supreme Lord Kṛṣṇa to sit there, then think that you are offering Him a nice cloth to wear and food to eat. Just by thinking of this it is not false. Kṛṣṇa will accept an offering like that. He said this is meditation, not the empty-the-mind sort of meditation. But if you practice concentration, then think of the personal Lord coming to the throne in your heart and you rendering Him personal service. Chant His holy names.

This is the narrative. But you think of this and that, and your meditation breaks. All small breaks and restarts. Return to the present moment and then again go to the life of the mind which is private. Each of us has his private mind, his own world. This is the person I want to appeal to in my writing. Say, "Here is a book for the private person." I'm not rebelling against public persons, but I am not so much addressing them. Everyone else seems to be addressing him, the social and public person. I am addressing the hermit in each one of us. Or put it this way: I am writing the life of both the inner and the outer, which each of us has to live. It is okay to talk about this, and even better when I actually enter it in my own case. I want to be sure that "you" are with me and understand all this. But you are certainly able to understand it and you wish me to take flight.

⁘ ⁘ ⁘

It is now 12:49. The time of the mind has no clock or mental version of it. Dreams should be told, not explained. Just little bits. Don't bore the reader seems to be my first rule. You want to be accepted so much. You ought to also be able to tell the reader, "I'm just doing what I want to do. If you don't like it, get lost, go somewhere else. Read your newsletter and bestseller."

Then go on your merry way, not as a begging dog wagging

his tail.

Hey Nannie, hey Nanda, hey son of Nanda, we wish to accompany You in the fields today. Please blow the bugle horn and chase away the dirt of our minds. Please allow us to be eligible to play with You. To tell you the truth, we are a little hungry from our play. We want the fruits of Tālavana, we want to beg a lunch from the feast of the nearby *brāhmaṇas*. But when the *gopas* ask these things, they were actually not thinking of their sense gratification, but of what Kṛṣṇa might want. Bhaktivinoda Ṭhākura says there are two kinds of persons in the world—those who want to please Kṛṣṇa and those who want to please their senses. Hey, Kṛṣṇa.

⁂ ⁂ ⁂

I remember I took guitar lessons but could never discipline myself to learn the songs by reading the music. Play a song like "Old Black Joe," or whatever. You prefer to fiddle around jazz improvisation. Ask the instructor who he thought was a good jazz guitarist. He said, "Tal Farlow." I started using the name "Tal" as my middle name since my own initial was T. Used it on the subscription form for "Downbeat" magazine. Another year I subscribed using the name Stephen Foster Guarino. You find it difficult to write this down and might prefer to talk again with the microphone. I just can't get much out here, want to say something else. Speak and get past the censors. The whole thing is to get past them … If you think you could express more by talking with a microphone, go ahead with that too. Just find a format as you did with your "Radio Shows." They were half-hour broadcasts running with the clock. You don't have that kind of time now. Maybe a shorter "truth" broadcast in which you do the same as here—a little of what's happening in truth (facts), and then beyond, make it up.

Truth broadcast

9:30 A.M.

If you're not obliged to do diary facts, you could write something else. But neither do I want to *forbid* myself to write the facts. Just go with it right now. Today not much desire to write or record at all. Maybe I'm a bit stunned by coming into the presence of so many devotees at the festival. The presumption of some teaching others. The ingrown nature of it all. And why should I not fit in?

Why do I have to fit in? I felt a headache was dissipated when I took a pill at 6:30 A.M. But then I thought it better to drop out of the rest of the morning program. That's leaving me feeling out of touch. I don't strongly identify with what's going on here.

Where would you rather be if not here?

July 2, 1996

Man dancing away alone in Fritzberg

3:00 P.M.

When I was in the temple in the morning my mind found fault and was uncomfortable in many ways. Later it occurred to me that the fault is in my own perception of things. This is an obvious point but I want to remember it and keep it actively in my mind. The devotees may also be imperfect, but that does not mean that the whole *saṅkīrtana* movement and all of its arrangements are null and void. The Deities in the temple, the temple worship, the effort to come together and have classes and *kīrtanas*, the sincerity of so many persons in spreading Kṛṣṇa consciousness—if all of this is glazed over by my sleepy, irritated vision, whose fault is that? If my heart is pure, I'll be able to experience Kṛṣṇa consciousness despite the real or so-called discrepancies of others and the arrangements they make for serving Kṛṣṇa and Lord Caitanya in this world. If I blame my own lack of focus on the devotees, on the Deities and on the spiritual master, then I become hellish. There's a lesson in *Caitanya-līlā* about this, in the behavior of the advanced devotee

Pundarika Vidyānidhi. Prabhupāda writes in the purport: "Pundarika Vidyānidhi saw that the priest neglected to wash the cloth before covering Lord Jagannatha. Since he wanted to find some fault in the devotees, he became indignant" (*Madhya* 16.78, purport). As a result of that hateful feeling, Puṇḍarīka's mind became polluted and that night the brothers, Lord Jagannātha and Balarāma, came to him and began to slap him. "Although his cheeks were swollen from the slapping, Puṇḍarīka Vidyānidhi was very happy within."

Swamis at festival

⁂ ⁂ ⁂

Read and be quiet or move along and do activities. You don't want to be alone all day. I stayed away from the *S.B.* class because of a headache. Now, I'm getting ready to give my own class which is scheduled from 4:00 to 5:00 P.M. I've given these Prabhupāda excerpts before, but the main thing is to feel at ease and to find within myself the actual *bhāva* for praising Prabhupāda and deriving lessons from the things he speaks. If when the excerpt plays, I feel an emptiness spread into the room, then I step in and just speak the best I can. Be detached. It's not that I have to drum up some false *utsāha*. Do what you can, what comes to you. The tape excerpts are wonderful in themselves, and this audience wants to improve themselves. Give them a writing exercise and don't grumble that you get a hundred papers to look through later. It's your bit. You will come alive from this.

Your private man benefits from public appearances. He can learn by being with others. Give yourself in this company. Hare Kṛṣṇa Hare Kṛṣṇa, Kṛṣṇa Kṛṣṇa Hare Hare / Hare Rāma Hare Rāma, Rāma Rāma Hare Hare.

⁂ ⁂ ⁂

As for writing itself, it has to come from the Vaiṣṇava source. You are not always a devotee. I know that. You remember bad things if you open the manhole cover. But you are not American or rhubarb pie. You don't think like that. Don't complain. There is nothing to be gained. You would like to sing and they are willing to wash the little clothes of your Prabhupāda *mūrti* and make him a little pie and you a big pie. Listen, you will go there and do it, okay? Say, "Listen folks, I listen every day to my own divine master and sometimes if I feel faultfinding, like Puṇḍarīka, I overcome it."

4:50 P.M.

Lecture Hall

I can apply the "something reading or writing, something reading or writing." Yeah, I want to do that all day. I'm writing now as the whole class is doing the assignment—looks like about seventy-five people and some standing in the hall too. Śacīnandana Swami is here and Navīna Krsna and Drutakarma. I did what I could. My repertoire of his tapes. If you've heard it before, don't stop me.

Then we'll go back to the house and see the mail which just arrived there. And then I have to look through their papers and choose some time for tomorrow. Next three days will be heavy with this.

I remember you, Swāmījī. I wish I did even more than I do. Please forgive my faultfinding mentality. I wish to be your *celā*, you know that. This is one kind of class. I tried to say things without being puffed-up.

I'm known as a big connoisseur of Śrīla Prabhupāda's sayings and moods. Big deal. it's true anyway, I'm an old-timer.

One man asked if Kṛṣṇa consciousness is simple or hard, and another asked, "Did Śrīla Prabhupāda see his disciples as angels or as quarrelsome?" I said, "Both, both, he saw us as both and still he gave us the medicine." No easy answer.

Something reading and writing.

It's such a nice thing.

Those coming to Kṛṣṇa consciousness were devotees in their past lives.

What was the thing he said that you can apply? They are writing, we have just three more minutes to go, then I'll collect the papers and try to make a quick exit. Don't expect to write much in the next few days. Okay?

Yeah, it's okay.

Something reading and writing—I mean it's okay to live alone in a loft and you don't have to go out. You can preach on your typewriter as he did, and read books. That's it—and you don't get tired, you do it twenty-fours a day. Hare Kṛṣṇa.

July 2, 1996

Inertia. Lost the ink flow from one day to another. My channel tunnel closed down operations. Couldn't sleep, then got up to answer some letters. Lay awake with a hot GBC paper on my mind. And the mail. Then went back to sleep and deliberately slept through the midnight hour which is really the hot line link. Since then, this July 3rd has been no writing for me. Of course, I live even when I don't write but I wanted to track July. And that subtle thread idea that you could forge (in the smithy of the brain, the conscience of the race) the truth of your little life, naming names and then you would depart for lies … it has wandered off.

But you can return to it. Writing like this has the most integrity when you don't perform for an audience. Just write for yourself. On the other hand, an impetus comes when you think it will be published. Better make up your mind.

I walked into the temple foyer and there was Jayapatākā Swami. I surprised myself by saying his name out loud, and then, "Do you remember me?" We both bowed down and I said, "It's Satsvarūpa from Boston." He said, "Do you remember Prabhupāda's arrival in 1969?" And he shot off some details of that. He was quicker than I was. I said, "Yes, it's never been outdone since then." Then some more chatter with disciples and younger devotees beheld us. Then we all went into the temple room. I was gingery with good footwork, but after all it was only for about a minute. You would never have lasted in a ten-round encounter with him. And not if some heavy issue focused on yourself was at stake.

The room was packed and stuffy. I sat against the wall and heard the lecturer with a British accent talking away on *śṛṇvatāṁ sva-kathāḥ kṛṣṇaḥ*. I have to lecture tomorrow so I try to think what to say then.

Two headaches today so far. In half an hour I go to give my second seminar lecture. That's it. A quick round up … But you have to be alone in your head.

Tomorrow I will read the verse where Vyāsa asked Nārada to tell of his life. I will tell the story of Nārada and then tell the life of Prabhupāda. And then I'll make my surprise and say, "There is another life we should be interested in. That is the life of each one of us." Go for it, wing it, like Ornette Coleman, go for it, say, hey man

we is each a soul
blow it baby
yeah, we should care, not that we are great
but it is not narcissism to see yourself.
It's you link with the world.

Try to find out who you are and how you're doing and how to improve. I could go over this with Madhu and track the ground I want to cover. That might be better than not preparing at all. Okay, but now hurry and go.

Once under a microscope a man saw a universe with green, pimply heads. The chief person was a poet potentate, a firehouse chief. He blew a horn … he listened to jazz despite their warnings …

⁂ ⁂ ⁂

This is July 3rd. I'm talking while I walk to the temple. We just left our house. Very busy now, not able to write in the morning. Far ahead on the road there's a light on and there's an entrance way which is to the temple. It's hard to describe, we're on a road that is not devotee property. The trees are on both sides and it's all dark. It's like being in a tunnel, and at the end of the tunnel you see the light. In this case the light is on under the arch, a big stone arch and it gives the effect of being in a tunnel and seeing a light at the end where actually you are outdoors and the tunnel effect is only an effect of trees. It is a memorable thing and that's why I wanted to capture it: this long, dark road where there's no light anywhere except at the end of the "tunnel."

⁂ ⁂ ⁂

The moon has been out for a few days as a full moon mostly covered by clouds. Now it's turning more fullish but oblong. In the temple there are many *sannyāsīs* gathered and it's a festival time. They also announced yesterday not to chant *japa* early in the morning—the neighbors don't like it. Maybe the cows like it though. Trees on both sides as I walk. These next three days will be hard-pressed to do any writing in my book, *The Faithful Transcriber* and I do wish to get to back to the life of a free-writer, a timed book writer.

I took rest last night and couldn't sleep. Got up and answered some mail. Now I should go and chant Hare Kṛṣṇa and be with the devotees in the temple. Say, hello, hello in your false teeth and your false demeanor and your true demeanor too. I made it yesterday but so much of what I see is false due to my own nonsense. So, try to see the Deities not as statues. Try to see the devotees not as ordinary people. Hare Kṛṣṇa Hare Kṛṣṇa, Kṛṣṇa Kṛṣṇa Hare Hare.

Another thing I wanted to say about this appearance is that after a while you realize visually that you are not in a tunnel, and can see just ahead big trees that look like a mountain over this archway. And in the dark you can't tell where you see the big trees because of the rough edges but still it's very strange and imposing and only to the right of it you see the outline of a chateau (which is the temple with trapezoid-ish shape of one roof and the other is like a chopped bonnet typical of Belgium here). ISKCON Chateau. At first you enter into the tunnel which is the arch under the big, big tree and then you look over to the temple. I wanted to tell you this, I wanted to tell you this so that you know what it's like to be here.

July 4, 1996

Tell them the life of Nārada. It's a partial bluff. You say you love it more than you do. The point is a disciple inquires into the life of the spiritual master because hearing of his life is as important as hearing the philosophy from him. I hear his life—after he met his spiritual master. He was bound by the affection of his mother. Professor Hopkins liked it too. But we believe it, it's not just "a beautiful story." His mother died. He went North in the life of a mendicant. Took water in a lonely place. Then saw God. Then heard Him. Then he wandered, satisfied, humble, etc., wandering, chanting.

Then I say—as wonderful as this is, yet it happened very long ago and only a few lines tell it here. But Śrīla Prabhupāda's life ... 26 Second Avenue. *A Lifetime in Preparation.* The centennial year is increasing our remembrance of him with many memoirs. The years before he came to the USA, his childhood, etc., are very interesting to hear. He said, "We took mangoes running in and out of the house." The best teller is Prabhupāda himself by his own memories, and here's a tape of him telling it.

I was thinking to say: our own life is a life also, to learn lessons from. We regret our past activities and remember what we have done in a fallen state and we try to join our life now to the life of the pure devotee. Join it as his servant. Mold your life to suit his pleasures. Join the line of Nārada. *Acyuta gotra.*

One man walking, another dancịng

In Rādhā-deśa I stake a little claim.

Walking back to the house where we stay. I missed a lot by not going on *Vraja-maṇḍala-parikramā* all these years, but nothing, nothing about writing this way, whatever comes. Bhakti-mārga Swami is walking all across Canada from west to east, equaling two Govardhana *parikramās* per day. Then why don't I stay in one place and just write while M. gets this van registered once and for all?

Man pointing

But it could take a month. Maybe we should go back there as soon as possible (Ireland) and get it done via the tunnel. That ride. But I want to see you writing or reading, something writing or reading. If could you live in the van, like a tinker, even that would be nice.

Join your life to his as his servant.

Dig alone this life of writing. Do I dare change the format of *PMRB*?

How I came to Kṛṣṇa consciousness is a wonderful story. Now finish it and complete it successfully. The life of Prabhupāda in 128 chapters of 100 volumes. You hear it and merge in it and learn from it how to be a pure devotee of Kṛṣṇa. After he met his spiritual master, he molded his life, "I have met such a nice, saintly person." Hear from him then. Wrote *BTG*. And finally arranged to go West and then back to India to open great temples.

The Faithful Transcriber. He bats away at the typewriter to tell his story now in July. As quick as possible the truth. We are staying in a nice house. It is comfortable. But soon it will be time to move on. You wear out your welcome. Mr. Guarino has to register this van sooner or later to get the right license plates. It is the important thing to do in the world. And he has to tell the story that goes with it.

I remember I was a hippopotamus in a zoo and I ate raw carrots. They came out of me.

The Surrealist Game Book is in the van—I didn't get a chance to look at it. I have no time. Give me something full-time to write while you are working on the van. This is maybe what we should do and only after it is done, then we are free to wander outside Ireland. That's one way to look at it. You have residency for a year to live in little Ireland.

I dreamt there were rituals in Ireland and although the

pious people were ridiculous and bureaucratic, I favored them over a tall, hippie-like atheist who uprooted the trees that had just been planted as part of the rituals. We wanted to stop him from doing it.

Go ahead, distract him, stop him.

Read only Kṛṣṇa conscious books? Keep the straight and narrow path and be satisfied with it. Eat only healthy food.

Well then you better take that stuff out of the letter, asking for Ornette Coleman and Paul Desmond. But if you think they really will help … you listen and then play the tape and go for it.

You see, that extreme is not what you are after, but a simple life. Yeah, but an American should do something wonderful for Prabhupāda.

What does that mean? It doesn't mean to listen to jazz, it means: be a wonderful, simple soul and live on a Kṛṣṇa conscious farm or distribute many books. Everyone can chant Hare Kṛṣṇa, I said. Although not everyone can distribute books or live in a temple or give money or so on—everyone can chant. I emphasize it's not the *only* thing but it is essential, the chanting of the holy names. I didn't say it so directly.

Jazz is incidental. Some leftover karma. The thing is to go alone and write as much as possible. But can't you cut through and see what it is you should do in art form?

Natalie Goldberg says maybe, but maybe it's best to just let the hand keep moving and take you where writing wants to take you. The break-down. The writing until you reach your subject and then you keep going with it although your heart gets heavy.

This is a little space before the day starts. There will be more spaces but you have letters to answer and even more than that, the presence of many devotees at this festival. You have to keep up appearances. This is one week. Then next week in the same place there is a different scene, disciples' meetings, two a day for four days. After that you get released. I want to see you keep up something while this goes on. Call it a book, a snook, a dook. But what is the point for writing something more than a book? It's the direct cut, the cut to the bone, of what you need to say and all that. Hare Kṛṣṇa, Hare Kṛṣṇa, what's your mission, bud?

4:50 P.M.

Lecture Hall

I just gave the writing assignment: "Do you find anything dry in Kṛṣṇa consciousness? If so, write how you may overcome this." I find it dry when I can't hold the audience and sometimes the philosophy goes on too long. Sitting too long at *Vyāsa-pūjā* homages. Remedy: maybe just avoid them.

Answering letters, *sometimes.*

I remember one devotee wrote on this question that he found everything dry at certain times, so he varied from one service to another.

Chanting rounds. Rounds are like that.

Leaders making political or too managerial talks, pushing their point of view or long announcements after *maṅgala-ārati.*

I'm sorry I feel that way.

Writing this with pain. So, let me take my fourth pill of the day. You needn't ask Madhu. It's up to me. Four in one day is not good, but it hurts and I want relief. "Extended and repeated use of this medicine is not recommended." But S.R. said, "Go ahead, take four in a day if you need to."

Dry, dry. Please Lord, although I find Your holy names

dry, I don't want it that way. Even if it must be dry, at least let me pay attention anyway and persist. Even saints feel dryness.

July 5, 1996

Last day of the seminar, then I get two days off before beginning four days of disciples' meetings. Yesterday headaches coming back again and again. I gave an *S.B.* lecture and my afternoon seminar. Not enough time to write here. The expectations of a book, a book. *The Faithful Transcriber* tells the truth and nothing but the truth but such a small amount of it. And … Allen Freed rock 'n' roll.

Dream: we were crossing a big expanse, dangerous. Wanted to hear jazz on the radio, but you couldn't because ears had to be open and alert. Wild elephants might attack. We saw them in the distance with antagonistic owners on top. To get over the last miles in safety I took help from an unpopular girl (put it that way). Held her hand and she got me into the last bend in the river where we were finally safe. In dreamwork terminology I thought this girl was a part of me not usually honored and that she can help me when I need it. Don't be too proud to refuse help from the sub-persons. It's not that one sub-person only—the Writer or the Devotee—is taking across, but all can help in their way. Although it was too dangerous to listen to jazz during that crossing, there may be a time for that, or at least you have to listen to that need and say, "What is it you so persistently want and how we can fulfill it in a Kṛṣṇa conscious life?" Nothing should be indulged in to hinder us in this life from our goal of attaining BTG, or at least going as far as we can before life is over.

Alarms and reactions. The worst is coming, as karma. ISKCON *sannyāsīs* tap into doomsday predictions and as a result devotees stock up on extra dahl. Sounds amusing.

Oh, depend on the holy name, it's all we have. Publish books while you can.

They said, oh, when he died, we saw how quickly people washed their hands of the departed and got on with life. That's the way it is. We just want to live and damn the dead, let the dead bury the dead. But if someone can leave books (and drawings) maybe we have something to remember him by. Ray Carver and Machado, etc. live in their poems a while.

Yeats and Joyce on the money.

Did ya hear? We are going to head back to Ireland as soon as these festival days in Belgium are over. So, be here another week. I think and ride on. In Ireland I may end this book. Until then, I won't have fulltime on it, but still, dear reader, dear Manu and friends, don't desert us. We'll give you news of events we couldn't give even in a one place retreat. Here we are in ISKCON, interacting intensely, so if we don't get too irritated by all this, we will give you little flashes … in between answering mail and lecturing. Giving heart in person to people who seek it. A lady wrote me about her doubts in her guru. I told her to pray for him. She came up to me yesterday and thanked me for that, but still it was man and woman. I'll be glad to be away from all that and in a snug place to write. You, you are fine people. The gurus and their disciples. The GBC fiercely protecting its flock. The … clock submerging it all in sands of desert time so that today's pressing concern soon becomes an old issue and one wonders if he's dealing with what is actually timeless or if he's tricked by *māyā* into the short time concerns. Don't say Śrīla Prabhupāda didn't warn you.

One man carrying another

To get through the day and offer inspiration to others. Do I belong in this fair-skinned European area where people are gathered to hear about Kṛṣṇa? The leaders and congregation. Jayapatākā Mahārāja, for example, is saying that there are thousands of devotees to be gathered in *nāma-haṭṭa* preaching. Just because they don't live in a temple doesn't mean they are not devotees. I wasn't aware that is his special interest. I supported it and said just because they don't live in the temple doesn't mean they are not very good devotees. Balance and praise and carry on. Please excuse me. I will write a note to the speaker of the day's *S.B.* class, explaining that I will not attend, got headaches all day yesterday. That note will be okay. And then all day I'll be able to cool it and try to recover from yesterday. Then if you feel better, maybe you can attend class tomorrow when you don't have your own lecture to give in the afternoon.

Those who expect so much of you. They want to see you sing and dance. They want to read a book by you. They want you to go to their temple and in various ways fulfill the purport of the verse: *nikuñja-yūno rati-keli-siddhyai.* Show yourself at least the perfect representative of Śrīla Prabhupāda. Do it, do it.

I say to you, heaven and earth shall pass away but the words of Christ and Kṛṣṇa shall not. True enough. And the footnotes. The sojourners can break loose into more thoughtful reflection. I ought to chant, he keeps saying, giving you the impression that he really doesn't have time to write. But if he did, it would feel so boring—a useless endeavor, pushing a big ball of straw across the field. "Why am I doing this?" he calls out, but he can't stop now. The *pāda-yātrā* has been announced all over the world and they're expecting him to go on it and to show up and to cover the miles on blistered feet. You said you'd do it. *Pāda-yātrā* marathon. I'll give you another chance later.

July 6, 1996

12:34 A.M.

I heard TKG is mostly staying in the temple in Dallas and pursuing "his studies." When I heard it, I thought, "Studies? In Prabhupāda's books?" Then I recalled hearing elsewhere that he's attending the university. So, he's fully into it and only travels during the summer. He told his disciples it's the best preaching he could do and it's best for them. Told them they have to fly from the nest. I heard it and thought too that I too have a right to pursue my studies as full-time as possible. I attend the university of writing in the notepads, writing. Then I heard that the anti-cult movement in France is growing bigger and the government declared ISKCON a dangerous cult and in Germany the government denied our religious status on the grounds that our philosophy is against democracy. This news had a similar effect on me, somehow, as the news of TKG's studies. Write, write. Write it down that you are afraid because ISKCON is branded. Go with the emotion it creates. When I feel pain or fear it is another kind of adventure, like a dream. Or—to cope with the anxiety that ISKCON is branded, you turn to writing.

Someone wrote me wishing that I have good health, tasty food (maybe good walks too) and that I find time to happily write without caring for the audience. Run into that space. A quiet meadow, where you meet the void and your own demons. And you write through it in victory. Victory celebration in Bhaktivedanta Manor, Prabhupāda disciples' reunion, whatever I hear—*pāda-yātrā* across the country—becomes another metaphor for the writer's life. A fellow my age said he is just coming to Kṛṣṇa consciousness, read a few of my books and liked them. But he wrote to me that I'm too hard on myself. He said Prabhupāda loves me and I love him, but he saw lamentation and void in my writing and asked me to give up the lamentation. He said, "You caught the wave (of meeting the Swami in 1966) and you are writing it and you are beautiful." He said he is coming so late to Kṛṣṇa consciousness and regrets it but doesn't lament. I wrote him back and said, "Yes, maybe my lamentation is a material thing, or maybe it's spiritual."

Unsteady—whether the pills can check the headaches. Not forever. The body is running downhill and picking up speed. Write while you can. So, we are fixed on returning to Ireland in a week. Hope to be there and write without disturbance.

Oh, read, my lad
read of Lord Caitanya at
Puri and go there some day,
write of His love
for all devotees
and the spreading of the holy name
where even the *mlecchas*
became ecstatic and chanted Kṛṣṇa, Kṛṣṇa, Hari.

No more Guarino although his name is appearing more on Irish forms. May he too join the effort to write, our study.

Now, soon you'll be chanting.

Proofreading *September Catch-all*,[1] when we four took a

1 The book being referred to here is *I Am Prabhupāda's Servant: September Catchall*, published by Gītā-nāgarī Press (GN Press) in 1996 as the third volume in the Books Among Friends series. It was written between August 30 and September 30, 1995. Only 100 to 200 copies of each of the Books Among Friends were printed.

sixty-four round *vrata* for seven days. Can you do it again? Yes, but I don't know when. The holy name rose predominant. We asserted its importance in our lives and put aside other priorities. Chant now at least your sixteen in good time.

That's all I can afford.

Two days off here and then four days of disciples' meetings. I'll be able to report a little in between, how the meetings are going and any excess steam or insights.

And some say bad karma is coming soon to the whole planet. But Prabhupāda said to keep working to spread Kṛṣṇa consciousness as best. When Kalki comes or before that when some of our preaching facilities close down, you'll be forced to stop. Until then, write it as best you can.

⁂ ⁂ ⁂

You say you want to write a lot in the upcoming weeks without so much outside input, but you know what that means. You'll have to face the page with nothing to say because you are not writing a story with structure. You are going into the unknown, in the layers of self, with fear that it may not be a Kṛṣṇa conscious thing. You'll have to do that to persevere. Sam Beckett be damned. The mind be damned. At least I'll be reading only Śrīla Prabhupāda's books and not listening to non-Kṛṣṇa conscious music. I'll be going on whatever I have. You have a whole life of Kṛṣṇa consciousness in a little thread, like your blood in the veins coming through to you.

My dear disciples, my dear Manu, dear mother, dear Irish government and cows and bulls for slaughter, and head, precious head, *kīrtanas* I didn't attend. The walks … You'll be writing for no audience and yet …

So, it is not like it will be all a big feast or you know

what you are doing. That is precisely it, you have to enter the wall, the blank and the uncertainty and you just keep writing anyway. I have a little book, *Surrealist Games*, but they have a program of their own, don't they? The mind, the unconscious. I will look for rational in the irrational, for art in the scribble. What seems to me to be sometimes too much self-absorption. A fellow who likes to write and draw wrote me and said some devotees accuse him of being idle for writing all day. He said, "How to justify it as preaching if you don't publish?" I told him to write for purification, but it's hard to convey. You have to go ahead and depend on Kṛṣṇa, *Un Poco Loco* too, with hope that will be your offering. But I think if going to the university is Kṛṣṇa conscious, then so is this. I just have to make it come out right from a Kṛṣṇa conscious life. Writing is a mirror reflection of an actual life.

Happy about my little private edition books like *Upstate* and *June Bug* and *Dublin Pieces* and so on. They are a genre-like short stories. In these last days I'll answer as much mail as possible, clear the way for writing days ahead in July and August. Please forgive me, *Faithful Transcriber*, if I am now turned mostly to what will come after you are completed. You are a bridge. Each book is that, provides me a way to go. I believed in you and later gave you up? No, this book is true adventure, the coping to get through these days and hoping that a book can come, either this or the next. This one has the characteristic of more overtly wanting to be a book and also dealing with outer events in ISKCON. I'm not a recluse but here at Rādhā-deśa. Put it forward as proof.

This is earning me the right to do the other, to declare, "I'm going to write." Forever. Forever is just a little bit of time on this earth. No one is stopping me in the summer of '96 from this Centennial offering, this gathering of water from 108 rivers and putting it in the pen with flavored ink stains. Kṛṣṇa is allowing you. Kṛṣṇa, who appears on the horizon (one devotee wrote) "in gargantuan form across the whole horizon"—his poem was called "A Soul's Smitten" and expressed his newfound love, falling in love with Kṛṣṇa consciousness, a young man in Manhattan.

I have the privilege and want to reciprocate as best I can in this way. Please forgive me. Don't forget to schedule reading of his books. Don't go off the deep end. But have courage on this inner journey.

4:30 P.M.

Headaches, temple attendance and lecturing by me are making it impossible to sustain this book. I get just one shot a day at midnight. Or whenever I get up. That's how it will finish out except maybe the two days travel from Belgium back to Ireland.

Turning also to the extended writing time in Ireland. But I should know that what I set myself up for will be only a beginning and I'll have to find my subject—if any—by writing.

Sometimes it may be a structure you stick with but maybe you shouldn't even try.

July 7, 1996

Ratha-yatra in London and Paris. Which are you going to? I'm staying here. "I get headaches." Faithfully tell your truth. Under veneers, strip away. Tell the truth. If you don't worry about censors, you can go a long way *in, in, in.*

I'm not going to the Ratha-yātrā
my stomach growls.
I want to see Lord Viṣṇu.

I want to write honestly even if it's not always KC.

In a dream, Kim Knott was lecturing on her role of defender of freedom for small groups such as people who chant Hare Kṛṣṇa.

I read some in the book *Surrealist Games.* Realized I'm not much committed to trying to destroy the individual's talent or to be a rational, to worship chance, to be a reverend, to write in an automatic way to shortcut discursive language, etc. I see the use in that but I do have something significant to say in delivering Kṛṣṇa consciousness. My purpose or interest in some methods of Surrealists might be (as in free-writing) to get past my censors and not say things in same ways that has become half-dead by use and familiarity.

But not just change for change's sake.

You've got a message?

Go to Uddhava's, work in the attic and sometimes in the outdoor room he has in the garden, and work steady in writing exercise manner. How will it be different than that series of many writing practice sessions I did there some years ago in the summer? They didn't have any theme and they ended in my becoming tired of them and finally wrote *Progresso*[2]

2 *Progresso: A Ten-Day Book Seeking Kṛṣṇa Consciousness*

in ten days. I don't know what the difference be. Can't give you a guarantee. The "guarantee" would be to think ahead of a "story," theme, etc. and then follow it. But you say you want freedom. Freedom also means staring into space and writing into it. Trust you'll go somewhere if you just go and explore.

The heart's truth rather than try to please (or make publishable).

Will something like that even come up or is it just a truth of humbly writing down little things? Look at Last Days of the Year, 1994.[3]

It's a road,
bridges
streams to cross
it really is your *pāda-yātrā*
and this is what you meet.

You are writing right now of what it will be like in a week. But what is it like now? It's okay. Belch and sigh. Today "everyone" is going to Ratha-yātrā so I don't have to go either to the temple or to the RY. Stay in this house. I've answered the mail, I am mostly prepared for the four days of meetings. So, I can do what I like in this one day. Read some *Cc*. Maybe take another shot here.

⁂ ⁂ ⁂

---

was written between August 6 and August 15, 1994, and was published in 1998 as the tenth book in the Books Among Friends series by GN Press.

3 *Last Days of the Year, 1994* was written in December 1994 and published by GN Press in 1999 as the eleventh volume of the Books Among Friends series. In 2021 it was republished as *Last Days of the Year* for the GN Press SDG Legacy Project.

The word "cult" is sticking in my brain from the anti-cult propaganda. Made destructive cults and the bad name they give us and the governments branding us. Let me, let us not get bogged down by those fears or disapprovals. Hṛdaya is worried it could affect their tourism program in this temple. Kṛṣṇa consciousness means to give people Kṛṣṇa consciousness one way or another.

Don't be afraid to wear *sannyāsa* clothes and *tilaka*. Tell people about Kṛṣṇa. Let them at least see you as a devotee. Pray? Yeah, why not? But did Śrīla Prabhupāda say that? He so much emphasized *more* than a silent, enclosed prayer to bring others benefit. Go out and chant loudly to them. Place a book in their hands, etc. But God is the great mover in people's heart. You can pray to Him.

It will be nice in a trice.

I'll go my way.

M. is working on the van. Sometimes you wish he'd pay more attention to this inner literary world. But it's good too—as he turns enthusiastically to his van work and workers helping him, I may take it as a signal that I should turn to my world of writing—as that is a lone world.

I have the privilege to do it. I have the opportunity many don't want to have. "A writer? Fantastic! I wish I had time to write."

Go do it, Mr. Blake, Mr. Hive. Go create your world of Kṛṣṇa conscious writing.

And how will it be used?

It may be used, I'll tell you. Free-write taps into "unconscious." We want to do that, not just for its own sake to see dream monsters and oddities and puzzles unsolved. Keep going to a truth—do you see it may be dangerous?

"At last, the words of truth are torn from deep in his heart, the mask is removed and reality remains."

Homely, homely reality.
Don't be so hard on yourself,
wrote Max Perry to me.

But it's a question of truthfulness, not whether I feel good or bad.

You think catching words from the periphery will help?

Yes, faithful transcriber and also reaching out for them. But more than that.

⁂ ⁂ ⁂

Imagine, imagine

the facts beyond your prose and beyond your own life. Fiction and fact meet there. Where? That "transcriber" and the "lies" —remember that program? Write your feelings and you owe nothing to reality.

In and out at any moment, changeable like the weather.

⁂ ⁂ ⁂

"Which Ratha-yatra are you going to?" he asked.

I said, "Oh, I'm giving disciples' meetings the next day so I am staying back."

Then he said several times, "You must go see my shop, my store."

I said okay, but why should I? What's the point? What do I owe him or anyone?

Why don't they come and read my books? I could say, "I will go to your store if you read my book." But I don't say that. I'm okay.

I'm a person. I am ten persons.

I am writing a book. After these four days I will have had

quite a dose (eight meetings) where I am myself the guru with disciples. That will be a good time to get away for writing. If they will let us over their national borders and we can go where we want to go. It is all right to go to the same place and write the same thing because as the Greek (was it, Heraclitus or Pythagoras or Plato?) said, "When you step into the river you never step into the same place twice." It won't be the exact same. There will be flies in the backyard and he and his wife will come to tend their garden frequently and that may break some of the solitary nature of your trying to write. Those things are common factors, you may feel free to write in the hermit's life. Okay?

First, these days of disciples' meetings.

Hello, dear disciples. I am training you to be such-and-such. I am trying to leave you and go to write. That is what is really on my mind. No, don't project that, "I'd really rather be somewhere else," but give them in those hours that you are with them. It is all right that you are ultimately detached from it. That adds to your spiritual offering, if you can do it rightly. You don't have to be lovey-dovey, but you feel obliged to be with them. They supposedly like to be with you and respect what you give. So, give it. It may not touch your heart utterly, but maybe writing and being alone doesn't do that either. Only Kṛṣṇa can do that. And, do you show yourself sufficiently interested in Him for Him to reciprocate that way?

Eight classes, young faces. Another thing is I am changing within the process of writing. Maybe I don't believe as much in the idea of "first thoughts are best thoughts." I don't have to be obliged to the sounds of words, or the play of them, or just because one floats up on the stream. But neither do I want to too carefully think something out.

Could you do a different kind of work? Look, no one can do this for you. You were going to write a book *In the Back of the Van* but the back of the van isn't ready. That's an example. So, write where you actually are instead. Then you thought maybe you could write something witty and fictional about the fact that you had to prove to the Irish government you are Stephen Guarino and get residency in Ireland on the basis of being a religious writer. You actually did that one day at the justice department but you didn't get much mileage out of it in writing. You wrote instead a *Geaglum Diary* and that data is preserved.

What actually is and was: the hawthorns in bloom, big pleasure boats on Lough Erne, the split in your energies between *Poor Man Reads the Bhāgavatam* and diary and finally backing out of *PMRB*.

Oh, you did that. Gave up *PMRB*? But wasn't it good to be so close to *śāstra*? Yeah, it was. But it was no longer gelling or organically satisfying as I felt it had been for the first fifteen hundred pages. You don't expect me to write my whole life that way, do you?

The dare I have thrown out to myself is—do you dare to change the structure of *PMRB*? That one will have to wait a while.

July 8, 1996

12:59 A.M.

Struggling with headaches. No time for a full shot writing session now. The four days of disciples' meetings are here. At the first meeting, I'll tell them I'm taking allopathic medicine to rise to the occasion of each class—so, they shouldn't be puzzled why I say, "I get headaches every day" and yet they see me giving classes. Let the cat out of the bag. But now even the pills don't check the headaches sometimes. So, they'll know if I have to cancel. M. said it's enough that they did the *tapasya* to come here and me too. Now whatever we can exchange, that's good.

Start with a vital topic of our relationship and draw from letters from Śrīla Prabhupāda. So, you are claiming a guru relationship with them. You expect to do this for four days and nights and then leave it behind and feel and write like a humble solitary? Well, I'll write about it too if necessary.

A guru went on *pāda-yātrā* with his disciples. They set up places for him to lecture but he bagged the goo. He wrote, that is, even chance nonsense as it occurred to him and until his pen time ran out.

He walked and press reporters did not besiege him but occasionally one did and he said, "We are chanting for peace." Fictive joy and Adidas sneakers, sixty-four rounds and the mind on its own *pāda-yātrā.* Big balls of mercy and dust sagebrush from the plains and kids in cars almost ran him down, shouting, "Ferbusher!" What's that? He didn't know but returned to his rounds.

Break out of confining.
Answer letters, sing Hare Kṛṣṇa
take one thought after another,
sing a memoir but I don't
like to extend them. Just bits

and pieces as you go along. And select, select. Crows land in the present and cows doomed on that hillock at Uddhava's and the little house crowded with paraphernalia by Madhu and his phone calls and saga with van and bureaucrats. You know all this will occur and nothing will stop you in your writing marathon, keep the hand moving. Keep broom sweeping. Rains of mercy frequent in Ireland. Let those clouds be fresh and cleaning the soul.

He walked out and it was okay.

Pray to get through this day with your scheduled program. Pray to be sober and instructive and human and dulcet-toned and humorous. Human and Vaiṣṇava guru *paramparā*. Answer letters, typist can construct English grammar. Facts to publish books— "when you get money," is good for me too. Angel-ish; those who think they are especially spiritual. And others. Primrose, wildflowers with flies in them, chase them out of this room, lay me down to sleep and use this body a while longer before they lay it in the shallow hallow with appropriate last words. Divvy up belongings as Roman soldiers did with Christ's cloak. All glories to Christ and may we increase in knowledge of his actual example and person.

Learn from Śrīla Prabhupāda and Lord Kṛṣṇa all that is to be known. Lord Kṛṣṇa will teach you in the heart. I have a long way to go and will take more than my allotted years. Oh, if I could hear in love and serve to please Him, not myself.

Kṛṣṇa, Kṛṣṇa, Kṛṣṇa.

⁘ ⁘ ⁘

The book they picked up for me in Dublin, *Hermits: The Insights of Solitude*, by Peter France, ends with a chapter on "A Hermit for Our Time: Robert Lax on Patmos." Lax used to be Thomas Merton's closest friend. Now, for forty years or so, he has been living alone on a Greek island." He writes every day … This kind of solitude is necessary to Robert Lax because he is a writer and can only work when free from all distraction. Solitude is, for him, above all a working environment—the only one in which he can write. And his writing is, above all, a search for meaning. Insights come from time to time, and if he can work them into a language he can understand, he feels they may be of use or interest to others."

We're then treated to some writings from his journals which are all dated entries. Then there's a conversation with Robert Lax and the author of the hermit book. Lax says, "I don't feel at all embarrassed about being or thinking of myself as a writer. I'm not using the word as honorific term. I'm not a novelist or writer of mystery stories. I'm just a writer who writes what's in his mind. I've always been a writer in this sense."

Peter France asks him, "Do you write to discover what you have in mind?"

Lax replies, "More to keep it from getting away. I think that, from the moment, I usually know what I have in mind and I also seem to know that five minutes from now I won't be able to rediscover it unless I've written it down … I have this confidence that if I ever to manage to clear things up for myself I'll be helping to clear them up for other people, and if I put it in a language that I can really understand, and find simple enough to communicate to myself in, then some other people will be able to pick up on it...I need to escape distractions in order to do something which is not, I think, anti-social. I don't think I'd be comfortable with it if it was. We all need each other far too much for somebody to take off and do nothing or do something destructive... If you found something creative that you can do in solitude when you're alone then that really is good news for the whole world. Because they may not be ready for it yet but they may be at another time."

4:30 P.M.

I gave them a writing assignment based on Śrīla Prabhupāda wanting his disciples to do their service. If you can't do it then say so.

It's up to them now to write. And I'll springboard it too. Twenty or thirty people here. Girls grow older like wilting flowers. Men get pudgy and old. All die. So fast, it happens.

We keep busy. Robert Lax on Patmos and me at Wicklow, writing down what we can to make it clear. Writing, writing, you get carried away. This is the first time I've written since midnight. I have so little time for it.

P. Swami predicts epidemic diseases and nuclear war by the end of 1997. Śrīla Prabhupāda said in 1974 that there would be "awkward" reactions to mass cow killing. You kill in the slaughterhouse and the reaction is "dum! dum!" (sounds like bombs). Material energy slaughters you.

I tend to think optimistically that it won't happen. We will fix our van, get our Irish license plates, drive over La Shuttle to Europe and back when we want to and go on writing. You better write while you can in this lifetime.

And I will be letting them write five more minutes. Faithful transcriber. Door opens, a five-year old enters and sits beside her mother in a pouting, shy mood. I write on. My hand is an old hand at writing. Snack, give me a snack, pie—Mrs. Wagner's pie—we used to eat them while out playing, eat in between meals.

Oh, I'll go on writing *pāda-yātrā* when I leave here. But now play the role well of guruji without frills. Gather questions and mind you P's and Q's, maybe they will write: "I was aghast when you said I am a servant and want to get close to guru, but I'm afraid of blowing it by sentimental false service."

N.D. doesn't know what to write so I suggested, "Write something about your relationship with Prabhupāda and how it lines up with your relationship with your spiritual master." That's a good one. They write slowly. But it comes out. I mainly need to use up the time of these meetings. Now I can use their papers and read them a little at future meetings. I'd draw a doodle here but it's not the right place for it. Deeper, face dragons and dreams. Turn to Lord Kṛṣṇa and don't listen to jazz.

As I write Śamīka Ṛṣi comes into the room with his family, back from their trip to Ratha-Yātrā, England. I'll write if Lord Kṛṣṇa allows in my solitude or crowded place.

July 9, 1996

12:16 MIDNIGHT

Walking as writing. Or rather, a full day's writing as walking offered to Kṛṣṇa, just as Bhakti Swami is doing. Nowadays it's just a note early in the morning before the *real* day starts. I ask for questions.

One I got is:
"What causes your stress?"
One is,

"How do you make spaghetti?" When you were a little boy, did you eat it every Wednesday or what? I heard you had some conflict regarding jazz. Do it if you want, but don't tell us about it. What is it? Desmond cools you off?"

But it is better not to. Unheard melodies are sweeter. Walk the sweat off through the pores. Got enough to work off from what I've done and heard.

Lax said he was living in New York City when the answers to all the questions he heard were New York answers. So, he wanted to escape that. I guess I have ISKCON GBC answers to things and I want to hear—myself. I don't want to hear N.M. followers or anybody else, even the doomsday astrologers. Write, write, and if it helps someone, okay.

Data, data. This is what I want: to get alone. You'll be among people at Wicklow. Will four weeks be enough? Attend (or send note to) the all-Ireland convention and say, "I propose to write and live alone most of the time and only come out for certain things like these meetings."

Cree-ripe.

The modes of nature bear heavily down. You can't escape

it, but write down things that occur to you. Your doodles are permissible in your own book. If it is good, it will do good for others. If not, it will not last. Who will assure this?

A drawing doesn't always have to be clear as to what it is, at least not super-clear each limb or the intention of the people. You are trying to make something clear but you don't know yourself what it is, so how can the drawing—or words—be completely clear?

Are people willing to read unclear writing? Is what people want your ultimate goal?

Now fax, flax and lax ask him for the pax to nax. Got it?

Oh, disciples' meetings be blessed.

I was going to play *Kṛṣṇa* be blessed. But maybe a little of this and a little of that would be better.

Dare to improvise at the disciples' meetings. A little of *Bhatia-loka* reading with comment and a little something else. There are really few meetings so I don't have to worry how I will get through.

You mean a grab bag of potluck questions. We will start out in the hour and see where it goes. The first meeting dug up so much you could keep going on that for quite a while.

So typically, I would end this midnight session early and go look at what they wrote yesterday and find good things to comment on. Each one might yield mileage.

Oh, he is walking
she is talking

they are looking, someone is putting. It is an epidemic, a bomb and a bomb shelter.

It's no joke. All your writing could go up in smoke.

Are you willing to face the bad things in your dreams? Lately I half-wake from dreams and only imagine that I put them on the tape recorder. Then I go back to sleep. I'm not really up to recording most of it. Only a fragment. I do have to sleep and not merely recover dreams. I am more aware that I do a lot of dreaming while I sleep. Need to deeply rest. Don't want so much to get up when midnight comes. I think of reasons not to get up. That's not so enthusiastic, is it? That's how I am these days. The main thing is these two shots of meetings. Get rounds done and go to that room for meetings with the men and women.

See the doctor today after breakfast. Tell him that yesterday I didn't take any pills but I wanted to see you, thinking that I was in a crisis. But yesterday at least I was better. One day at a time.

July 10, 1996

This is the third day of the disciples' meetings. It's one in the morning. I had a difficult night, didn't sleep well, first a fly was bothering me then I felt some indigestion. When I woke, I was feeling depressed by these events of the night in which I was trying to get some peaceful rest. Here during the day, I am being honored as a spiritual master but at night I can't sleep and I fall asleep but have different series of dreams and as usual there is always so much danger in them. They scheduled too many events for me today. In addition to the morning and evening classes, they've scheduled me to attend a lunch with all the disciples at one o'clock. But I think it may be too much to ask because I have to make an extra trip there and back and I'll barely have time to get back again by four o'clock.

Madhu spent all day yesterday: over two hours driving one way and then back and it was all mostly fruitless. He went to some mechanic who promised to install a gas tank under the van but never did it. Maybe I shared his frustration too as I tried to sleep.

Nevertheless, I must persist with these disciples' meetings. They're going well and there's just two more days and then I'll be free to begin a fulltime writing retreat.

Right now, I'm feeling some pain in the eye which is unusual for such an early time of the day. I'm not about to engage in wordplay here to go beyond the diary but I'm going to get ready now to chant my rounds. This is the faithful transcriber who doesn't feel much energy for telling lies or making literature but he's reporting in for the future record. Hare Kṛṣṇa.

July 11, 1996

I just finished writing outline answers to questions from disciples. This will be the basis for the last meeting we'll have today at 10:00 A.M. Here's a sample of some of the questions and answers.

Q: Is it wrong to desire or feel the need for personal attention from the guru?

A: It's not wrong to want personal attention. But be patient. Develop a personal service relationship and it will come naturally. Don't be envious.

In answering this I'll go on to read a letter from a disciple saying how he felt so much reciprocation when rereading *Radio Shows.*

⁂ ⁂ ⁂

Dear Diary, I find it too tedious to write down any more of these questions. I already just did it and it would be redundant for me to put it here. Besides, I have limited physical energy. Mainly I want to get through this day. I have to chant my rounds now. Then one activity after another happens really fast today and it's very tight. I have to worship Prabhupāda earlier than usual, put him in the travel box and then by 10:00 A.M. we're supposed to be all packed up (Madhu has a huge amount of packing still to do). And then I go to the 10:00 A.M. class After that it's only a brief while before we have the 12:30 meeting to see a *gurukula* show and then 1:00 P.M. *prasādam*—which is a public affair with all the devotees together. And then departure at 2:00 P.M.

One of the questions was, "how did Śrīla Prabhupāda sing the Nṛsiṁha prayers? I would like to learn to sing it the way he did."

For the answer, I'll sing it the way I do, which is the best I remember of the way he did it.

8:30 A.M.

Packing. M.'s got several men doing last work on the van—fixing a strap so the typewriter can ride on a shelf, fixing something so the plastic cartons can be strapped securely. And emptying this house. He tends to time everything so it's all done by just the last minute. An old story with us.

"I'm afraid of change," writes G. dasi in a last letter I get. Tell her something from the philosophy and from my own view: Kṛṣṇa wants us to depend on no niche or situation except His shelter. Easier said … Guru's words, how weighty and paid for?

Go alone and pay and weigh,
relax, sigh relief, write
quickly and slowly.

Always looking for a future. This last meeting is a good chance.

I told M. I could prepare some more Śrīla Prabhupāda excerpts for classes or even seminars. Transcendental disc jockey. "You seemed to enjoy it?" he said." Yes, I guess so. Do I enjoy more going alone to write or is that a myth?

You have to face the blocks, and cotton candies. The afternoons when words don't come from a hole, just sparks and surfaces—the attic, the backyard, the misgivings, the things of ISKCON that pass through your mind.

In about twenty minutes put Śrīla Prabhupāda in the wooden box and pack it up with the other crates. He'll sleep as we travel.

July 11, 1996

I intend to track the last two days. True to the theme of the faithful transcriber, but not the imaginative flights, no creative lies.

Once there was a man…They gave him jam with hemlock in it. He dreamt recurrently of possessing false currency bills. Always. Try to pass off your money.

Hope they don't detain us at the border into England at Le Shuttle. They do a quick security check of the van and then "passport control."

Sir, I was admitted to England on May 31st for six months, and since then I've become a resident of Ireland.

Why would you want to do that?

To write books.

Oh, have you written one honestly and what's it about?

About Kṛṣṇa consciousness. *Rāja-vidyā.* I'm a guru. Don't call me in for more interviews to prove I'm the owner of the van. I'm tired of that.

Don't stop, we want to go write a timed book starting as a sigh and then a slow walk, building momentum. Don't know what it is, but that it is built on words.

1:15 P.M.

Watched the *gurukula* play—Sāvitrī got her husband back from death. Smiling bare-chested boy in short pants playing dead sat up and said, "Something strange happened!"—smiled beautifully.

Then they sang:
"Devaki, Devaki,
please don't cry
tears of a mother's eyes.
Kamsa will die

and Kṛṣṇa will appear
to dry up your tears
and relieve you of your fears."

Now lunch is late and we wait. I hope I don't get a headache and I hope the van operates okay into England. Ekādaśī. Seven-hour drive. It could be bad luck on Thursday afternoon. Chant Hare Kṛṣṇa and all will be well. It may be a bad time to travel but our purpose is to serve.

Devakī, Devakī. Chant Hare Kṛṣṇa as we travel. Beads in hands. Faithful scribe writes it down. Motorcycles. I'm in the back of the van, sitting out for the announced fifteen delay before *prasādam* is served. M. is threatening them that we will leave at 2:00 P.M. with or without *prasādam*.

Lord, please protect us.

The young king died, one year after his marriage. His wife brought him back to life. But then we have to die a little later.

Hooded Yamarāja held a white noose. We thought it was fun. Headaches? Death? Cross into England?

Flies back here like the warmth. Oh, angels. Oh, Devakī. Lunch is ready.

2:35 P.M.

Rolling along the dual-carriage way. Brussels ahead but we are going to the Channel. Yes, it was a nice Ekādaśī feast. On behalf of all the devotees I thanked Hṛdaya Caitanya for providing us facilities. Yes, they agreed. Then I went and washed my mouth at Bhadrāṅga's apartment and saw his yellow neem Gaura-Nitai and the Śrīla Prabhupāda from Vṛndāvana which used to be mine. Nicely worshipped now. A visiting lady brought her traveling Rādhā-Kṛṣṇa Deities for me to see. Bhadrāṅga's four-year old daughter kept holding up dolls and Deities for me to observe. Saw his computer. Then Madhu came to gather me into the van.

This is perhaps the jinx time, a Thursday between 2:00 and 5:00 P.M. and on Ekādaśī. Chanting and asking Lord Kṛṣṇa for protection. We are carrying two devotees from Poland. They'll get off soon and hitchhike. Three of us will go on to England. Hope to reach there at 8:30 or 9:00 P.M.

Restaurant friterie. Brucellas. Citroen. "Capital B" on the back of a car means "Belgium." Our van with Pennsylvania license plates. Reppel. Words I don't know but transcribe faithfully. Writing okay on a second pill of the day and therefore able to write this.

I answered all the questions. Be guru. Now sigh. Breathe in and out. Be writer. Be servant. Namur. Brouillard frequent. Loyers Caravans be careful of the winds. Andenne. Jambes.

Kṛṣṇa, Kṛṣṇa, say Ekādaśī rounds.

France

4:45 P.M.

Can you write while driving, riding, veering, wires dangling, flies that bite? Read gas tank, road of engine. You can write a little but don't expect to think deeply as to your purpose. Maybe better this way. Fixodent. Snyder. I said I would write whatever I see. Hold on for the ride.

Paris, Disneyland.

Sworn off all music but *kīrtana*. AA Twelve Steps. I need Kṛṣṇa to help me: "You are a special person so you can see my Deities. I know They are not dolls." I peered into the box and saw white marble Rādhā with a braid and red hand offering benediction and blackish Kṛṣṇa, a little like

Rādhā-ramaṇa of Vṛndāvana. Said something, "You are fortunate. So, why should you feel unhappy?"

Now, now, I said I'm not heroic. Poured out all up-to-date realizations for them. Anurādhā ruddy. Pale, bemused *japa-yajña*, little kids, widow washing out a white *sārī.* Gentle yard and genteel life, gardens, old Dutch *pūjārī* walking there, doing afternoon *japa.* It was a nice Ekādaśī feast. Dhass all right. Śamīka Ṛṣi visiting temples in Europe with his family and sightseeing. He wants to see the Vatican. I suggested Assisi.

You'd better get down to a hard-core.

5:10 P.M.

Two passport controls at Le Shuttle. The first one is on leaving France. A group of five young French girls with pistols and holsters and blue uniforms. They were not occupied until we came and so they stopped us. French girl talks with Madhu who speaks her language. They come into the van, open the medicine, sniff at Triphala. Bhakti-rasa tells them it's "herbal medicine." They delay us but I sniff fresh air in from the open window. They are young girls.

Then we go to the British side, immigration. He's a bit suspicious. I say that I'm an Irish resident. He says, "Oh, are you?" with an official suspension of belief. Worst of all he stamps my passport taking two spaces. That was a downer but I still have a good number of spaces. Enough to last to at least the year 2000 when the passport expires?"

⁂ ⁂ ⁂

Rolling on the motorway. Suspended in time. Not in Ireland, not retreat, last days of this timed book. Put the data here, a brief sketch. An hour earlier in England. Lynx Express delivery network (back of truck). But where's the lynx? In a zoo. Oh, April is gone and June too and July half used. I've got time still in purpose. Work your way into it. Ireland is merely the setting.

Cc.—surrender there. Lord Caitanya in Jhārikhaṇḍa forest. Sitting up front as Le Shuttle carries our van underground and I read some and talk with Bhakti-rasa some. Car ahead of us, a sprawled out British family. Young boy had two broken legs and uses silver-colored crutches. Grandma in the back seat. They're transporting lots of beer.

The immigration Britisher watchdog asked me, "Where were you?"

"Just Belgium," I said.

"What was the purpose of your visit? Business or pleasure?"

"Religious," I said.

"It was pleasure," Madhu added.

The guy was not amused, pleased, just being a watchdog. And the rat (with mustache) stamped two spaces in my passport.

Don't complain. Śrīla Prabhupāda went through much more. Devotees are risking their lives, hearts pounding as they cross alien borders.

Ayles Ford South. London. M20. Sunshine glinting down through the windshield. Lots of cars in both directions all flowing fast. At any minute …

I think I'll go to the back now.

Police siren pulls us over. I stay in the back. His voice sounds harsh, not friendly. He's doing all the talking. What's up? Will we have to go to the police station? I hope not. Our papers are in order as far as I know. My mind speculates.

Were we speeding? A ticket? The cop is really talking. Now he's left.

I went up front and asked what it was. Madhu says that he cut the cop off when Madhu was trying to get into a lane. The cop said he could see that we were lost because of the way we were changing lanes. So, he talked and talked, giving a lecture about how we shouldn't have done what we did. Then he said, "All right, lecture ended. So, where do you want to go?" Then Madhu told him that we were trying to get to High Street. So, he gave us directions and then he drove off and as he went by, he waved. So, nothing so terrible. He must have seen our American license plates but not thought anything much of it.

July 12, 1996

We arrived on the street of row houses where Guru-dakṣiṇā lives and it was certainly nice to enter that haven and be greeted by him and his wife and sister-in-law. I told our little adventures of crossing the border and being stopped by the police. The girls then told a little incident of their day when they to the market in London and bought mangoes. They told the proprietor, who was an Indian, that these mangoes were for their guru and they made him go through all the boxes until he picked out the very best ones. "He must have made benefit," they said.

Nobody knew that Guru-dakṣiṇā and the ladies had come back early from Belgium. They did so just so that they could be here and we could make out pitstop overnight. They're very kind to us in that way.

It was warm in England, compared to the chill of Belgium. Too warm in fact. I went to my cozy room which is a third-floor attic and the skylight was open and it was noisy outside. We were all tired and so it wasn't hard to fall asleep. I slept until 2:00 A.M.

If someone had told me when I began this timed book at the beginning of July that in two weeks we'd be heading back to Ireland, I wouldn't have believed it. Our plan was that after the seminars and disciples' meetings we would explore some more of northern Europe. The main reason we're returning is that we felt it was too risky to travel around over borders with our US license plates and refused registration in Ireland. But strictly speaking, there isn't anything illegal about it. That was sort of a triggering reason, but the generating reason was that I saw the opportunity to get back into a full writing retreat sooner than I'd expected. Surely the seminar and the disciples' classes fulfilled all the profile points I might need to make at this time to show I'm an ISKCON preacher. Therefore, the question was really left to me, "What do you want to do?" Nobody really seemed to crave me or need me somewhere else. So why not go and do what you want to do and what you think is your own best preaching and fulfillment? Therefore, the triggering incident of needing to get the license plates led to the generating incident of wanting to enter a solitary writing retreat. So, I may be less dramatic or less adventuresome to end the book which was going to be European travels, and get back to facing the "blank wall" writer's block ("why do I write") and all that in an Ireland retreat, in the sometimes too domestic Wicklow scene. But that's where I'm headed to meet that cutting edge of being a writer for Prabhupāda, blending the self-searching with the presentation of Kṛṣṇa consciousness. I'll have to face why I'm not writing *A Poor Man Reads the Bhāgavatam*, why I'm making a more groping search. I have a starting idea of a book, somehow based with a symbol of daily walking, like a man on *pāda-yātrā*, seeing how far he can go each day in truthfulness. But it's not much of a structure and may fall away once I really begin.

Today breakfast and early lunch here. Bathed Prabhupāda, dressed him in new clothes, put him in the box and then off we go for the five-hour drive. I'll give you some more travel notes as we go, as we spend the night as we plan it in Holyhead, Wales, just a short distance from the fast ferry. I'll continue the notes until we get to Ireland. Hare Kṛṣṇa Hare Kṛṣṇa, Kṛṣṇa Kṛṣṇa Hare Hare / Hare Rāma Hare Rāma, Rāma Rāma Hare Hare.

GBC
BBC
BTG
CDE
NASA
BIR, BIT, Murfits, Losen L.,
Heads Antwerpen. Andorfen. The list is endless.

Read some in *Our Original Position.* Arguments refuted and asserted. Me better button my lip. Play in my own sandbox where I am king or at least a child among others entitled (by teachers' freedom) to say I like sand because—whatever reason. Whatever I witness is not wrong. It is my feeling.

BNT, IRT, SIRT, SICC, BC, BD, X, the only way, last exit to Brooklyn, Selby. Junior. Monk. Junior. Stephen Hero, Childe Harold, Father Hicks, Madeline Morrisey, Miss Rheingold.

I am entitled, I tell you.

I am not?

The Lord decides. The chatter-chit-chat is at least not censored by anyone. Surveillance is up.

You are still afraid of a Grand Inquisitor? The author of the band book "agreed" to withdraw it from sales. He was forced but of the same opinion still.

But bosses have to uphold law and order and I as artist-petit do support them. Thus, I am an artist of the institution, although some rebels don't like that about me.

4:10 P.M.

Off the motorway, up towards Wales. Nuclear chimneys and big steel towers carrying cables, the earth is being used. We are speeding to reach our Holyhead spot which Madhu predicts we will by 7:00. We were stuck in traffic, the price we pay for a leisurely stay and feast-lunch at Guru-daskṣiṇā's place. Usually, we like to travel very early.

I answered some letters in the back. Up front now. Sunlight glinting off of the bonnets of cars. Saw a few wrecks. Copy down the license plates. Cart off the injured. Bird dead. Glass shards.

Guy ahead in a red convertible, top down having an animated conversation with his partner, not paying much attention to the road. I told M. when we arrive at Wicklow, I want to drop out of the news about registering the van and also not be involved in Wicklow community letter exchanges. The mail pack will come from the USA but I'll just pick a few things from it and leave the rest in rubber bands. Talked of how to maximize writing. Put the large electric typewriter in the room Uddhava has in his backyard. Hard writing desk in the attic and use the attic landing for drawing. Floor space there too for poetry books and newsprint.

I'm already feeling some come-down, anticlimax, boredom. There's excitement in traveling and mixing. But I wanted time to write. Now face it. At my request, a disciple went to London and picked up *Tristam Shandy* and *Portrait of the Artist as a Young Man*. What do I think I'll learn from them? I have my own style. Someone says the structure of Sterne's book is like a chess game. I certainly don't want that. I don't even know how to play chess.

Industrial towers. Smoke from factories, can't tell the difference between that and the clouds. M. passed someone up and they beeped their horn.

I said, "Is that what the policeman lectured you on yesterday?"

"No. I was indicating but he wouldn't let me pass."

⁂ ⁂ ⁂

"Sorry for any delay, Welsh office." Royal Air Force, sealand. Now signs in Welsh and Griffins and white muscle clouds high up. A blimp in the sky—I peer until I see "Toyota."

5:45 P.M.

Parked at last at a Shell service station before the ferry. We've got a bottle of water I can pour on my head in the A.M. and drinking water. Just now filled up on petrol. A little longer and then stop for the night. Look kindly at others and hope they look kindly on me.

A disciple asked Prabhupāda (just heard it on tape) about the origin of the *jīva* and if he can fall from the spiritual world.

Śrīla Prabhupāda replied, "Even Lord Brahmā or Lord Śiva can fall. We must be very cautious of Māyā." He answered the real concern, even if the disciple was looking for something else in the name of theological inquiry.

Air Serv. Car vac. Dyffryn Garage. Strictly No Admittance. Everyone here speaks English, me too. Smart Ferrari Collection. Do not use—

Hum of the petrol machine pumping gas into cars. All is self-service here.

Kṛṣṇa, Kṛṣṇa, Kṛṣṇa. Kids on skates, wear gloves and wrist protectors, hats, bare chests. I don't have to tell the exact truth and nothing but the truth regarding material details. Someone says whatever we write is within the material energy. But if I vibrate *kṛṣṇa-kathā*, Kṛṣṇa's names, that's transcendental.

When someone makes what I think is a significant

favorable remark on reading my books, I save it. Against the winter of discontent and inner and outer critics.

Now beach and sea. Gulls. Dylan Thomas. You said it. Holyhead to Ireland. Coastal park.

⁂ ⁂ ⁂

Now parked at the ferry terminal. M. has gone in to get out ticket for tomorrow morning's sailing. We're in a place that's a restricted zone. You can park there for twenty minutes. After that, they'll put a clamp on your wheel and it'll take a fifty pound fine to remove it. Friendly. Fences, barbed wire.

Aindra dāsa tunes get us through. Prabhupāda in layers. Hey man, don't clamp my wheel, we've only been here five minutes.

Madhu comes to the window and said he just got us on an earlier ferry for 4:00 in the morning. Okay, fine, let's go quickly to that writing retreat. Be there by 8:00 A.M. tomorrow.

⁂ ⁂ ⁂

This book begins and ends with the ferry. If at the beginning of July, you had told me that we'd be back in Ireland in two weeks, I wouldn't have believed you. I would have said, "No way. After the seminars in Belgium, we're going on to explore Germany and maybe Poland. It's a month of travel and meetings and so, a travel book. I'll be mixing fact and fancy on the road."

But we've been drawn back like a magnet of writing service. After doing the seminars and especially after the intense disciples' meetings, I thought I'd paid my dues and I could really do whatever I wanted. Nobody was clamoring for me to travel and show up at different temples. They were doing much bigger things, somebody said there was a festival in Poland that was "another Woodstock." Big programs, so what can Satsvarūpa add? Why not do the big thing that's at least big for him? And so, on the plea of registering the vehicle, we're going back as soon as possible, before I burst a gut, to write the book I have to. I hope it will be a good one.

And so, the book begins and ends with the ferry. The travel book ends, like last year's *Kārttika Lights*, with a hopeful homecoming, return to Ireland for four weeks of writing. Don't tell anyone. Get into it. Yeah, I know there'll be anticlimax disappointment. But I'm going to maximize writing time. And it will be Kṛṣṇa conscious too.

July 13, 1996

3:00 A.M.

As I write this, we're leaving our overnight spot and heading for the ferry which is just a few minutes away. We stopped around 6:30 for taking rest but somebody came at 10:30 and moved us up. We were in the way of a truck weighing spot. We found a quieter spot. The van isn't really fixed up, so Madhu had no decent place to lie down and couldn't sleep. I slept off and on.

I'm always anxious to get in the queue as soon as possible. Even if I have to go to the spiritual world and there was a queue, I'd be anxious so that it wouldn't have a long wait. But Prabhupāda already told me personally when I asked him in an airport whether passports were necessary for the spiritual world. He said none of that is required. You go instantly. But in the material world, everything is a perverted reflection. Chant, chant, chant.

You may remember, dear reader, that the fast ferry crossing of the Irish in the beginning of July was difficult because there's such a heavy enjoying mood on the ferryboat. Loud video games, rock music, and you're imprisoned wherever you sit to be facing a big video screen with sound provided, whether you like it or not. I'm somehow hoping that a 4:00 A.M. crossing will have less of an enjoying mood. They seem to think that people have no inner resources and can't sit still for an hour and a half without being titillated all over the place by sound and visions.

I proposed to Madhu that we eat our breakfast on the ferry as another diversion. Then we could sit in their cafeteria area and not have to look at a movie screen.

July 13, 1996

We're only about four hours or less from reaching Uddhava's house, if all goes well. That means I'll have most of the day for moving in, setting up books and typewriters and papers and then tomorrow—with a calendar charted out for four weeks—begin writing fulltime. My dear Kṛṣṇa, my dear Śrīla Prabhupāda, thank you for this opportunity to serve You.

Written on board the Stena Line ferry to Ireland.

Tolerable crossing. Music but the video was warped. Loud. High point was a waiter who came and gave us free orange tea and two kiwi fruits. Then he came back and squatted beside us and talked. He had read Śrīla Prabhupāda's books, *Śrī Īśopaniṣad*, *Bhagavad-gītā*, and *Path of Perfection.* He said he kept passages from those books pasted above the till so he could see them as he worked. Both M. and I spoke to him. He said his reading of the books was more *jñāna-yoga* but he would like to practice *bhakti.*

I said he could learn *karma-yoga* so he could do it while working. I advised him to chant Hare Kṛṣṇa mantra. He's very busy working his job but wants to visit a Hare Kṛṣṇa temple and get into meditation and maybe chanting. Now Madhu is speaking to an Irishman beside him and talking mostly diet, meat eating, Buddhism, etc. I had earplugs in for a while but I overheard triple about Paris Disneyland, a new Disney film (I don't have to repeat it all, I'm not an agent for Disney or *that* "faithful" a transcriber). Slap, slap, that stupid rock drum beat. I wouldn't mind if I never heard it again in my life.

Speed cars.

M. is telling they guy, "I'm fit in health even though I'm a vegetarian." Don't kill the cow, you fool.

"You never have a steak?"

Okay, I'm ready to get off this boat. The guy talking to M. seems more interested in joshing than anything serious. Power of prayer.

Heading for writing yajña

Acknowledgements

Satsvarūpa dāsa Goswami would like to thank Nitai Gaurasundara dāsa for sponsoring the publication of this book. He would also like to thank all disciples and friends who helped produce this second edition of *The Faithful Transcriber.* The following GN Press Book Production Team members assisted with the production and publishing of this book:

Reverend John Endler
Satya-sāra-devī dāsī
Kṛṣṇa-bhajana dāsa
Lāl Kṛṣṇa dāsa

GN Press Book Production Team, 2024

Books of Satsvarūpa dāsa Goswami

Biographies and other books about HDG A.C. Bhaktivedanta Swami Prabhupāda

Calling Out to Śrīla Prabhupāda (1988, 2nd edition 2022)

He Lives Forever: On Separation from Śrīla Prabhupāda (1979, 2nd edition 2022)

Here is Śrīla Prabhupāda (1992, 2nd edition 2022)

Letters from Śrīla Prabhupāda (1982)

Life with the Perfect Master: A Personal Servant's Account (1983, 2nd edition 2022)

My Letters from Śrīla Prabhupāda, Volume 1: With Śrīla Prabhupāda in the Early Days (1990, 2nd edition 2022)

My Letters from Śrīla Prabhupāda, Volume 2: You Cannot Leave Boston (1992, 2nd edition 2022)

My Letters from Śrīla Prabhupāda, Volume 3: I am Never Displeased with Any Member (2003, 2nd edition 2022)

One Hundred Prabhupāda Poems (1995, 2nd edition 2022)

Prabhupāda Appreciation (1990, 2nd edition 2022)

Prabhupāda-līlā, Chapters 1–8 (1981–1982), Single Volume Edition (1987)
Chapter One: Return to America, 1967 (1981)
Chapter Two: Seattle, September-October 1968 (1981)
Chapter Three: Opening a Temple in Los Angeles;
Chapter Four: A Visit to Boston (1981)
Chapter Five: A Summer in Montreal, 1968 (1981)
VI: One Hundred and Eight Rosebushes: Preaching in Germany, 1968–1969 (1982)

VII: Śrīla Prabhupāda in Latin America, 1972 / 1975 (1982)
VIII: A World Tour with Śrīla Prabhupāda, 1975; Zurich and New York, 1973 (1982)

Prabhupāda Meditations, Volumes 1, 2, 3, 4 (1990–1993), Volumes 1–2, 3–4, 5 (2022)

Prabhupāda Nectar, Volumes 1–5 (1984–1987), Single Volume Edition (1996)

Remembering Śrīla Prabhupāda, Books 1–6 (1983), Single Volume Edition (1992, 2nd edition 2022)

Śrīla Prabhupāda-līlāmṛta, Volumes 1–6 (BBT 1980–1983)
Volume 1: A Lifetime in Preparation: India 1896–1965 (1980)
Volume 2: Planting the Seed: New York City 1965–1966 (1980)
Volume 3: Only He Could Lead Them: San Francisco/ India 1967 (1981)
Volume 4: In Every Town and Village: Around the World 1968–1971 (1982)
Volume 5: Let There Be a Temple: India / Around the World 1971–1975 (1983)
Volume 6: Uniting Two Worlds: Around the World/ Return to Vṛndāvana 1975–1977 (1983)

Śrīla Prabhupāda Samadhi Diary (1997, 2nd edition 2022)

Śrīla Prabhupāda Smaraṇam: Photos 1966-1977 (2011, 2nd edition 2022)

Your Ever Well-Wisher (one-volume abridged version of Śrīla Prabhupāda-līlāmṛta, 1983)

Autobiographical

Looking Back, Volume 1 (2015), Volume 2 (2017)

Memories (1997)

The Story of My Life, Volume 1 (2012), Volume 2 (2012), Volume 3 (2014)

Devotional Service and Devotee Life

"Distribute Books, Distribute Books, Distribute Books!": A History of Book Distribution in ISKCON 1970–1975 (1982)

From Imperfection Purity Will Come About: Writing Sessions While Reading Bhaktivinoda Ṭhākura's Śaraṇāgati (1993)

Guru Reform Notebook (1986)

Memory in the Service of Kṛṣṇa (1990)

My Relationship with Lord Kṛṣṇa (1995)

Obstacles on the Path of Devotional Service (1991)

Truthfulness, The Last Leg of Religion (1989)

Vaiṣṇava Behavior / The Twenty-six Qualities of a Devotee (1983)

Vaiṣṇava Compassion (2001)

Japa Meditation

108 Japa Poems 2010 (2010)

Begging for the Nectar of the Holy Name (1992)

Day by Day: A Record of a 7-Day Japa Vrata (1995)

Japa Reform Notebook (1982)

Japa Transformations (2010)

Japa Walks, Japa Talks (1994)

Japa With Pen (1989)

Prayer

Dear Sky: Letters from a Sannyāsī (1993)

Entering the Life of Prayer (1989)

My Dear Lord Kṛṣṇa: A Book of Prayers, Volume 1 (2009), Volume 2 (2010)

Vandanaṁ: A Kṛṣṇa Conscious Handbook on Prayer (1990)

Reading

A Compilation of Excerpts from Bhaktivedanta Purports of Śrīmad-Bhāgavatam (1994)

A Compilation of Excerpts from The Teachings of Lord Caitanya by His Divine Grace A.C. Bhaktivedanta Swami Prabhupāda Along with Reading Notes (1994)

A Poor Man Reads the Bhāgavatam, Volumes 1, 2, 3 (1996, 1998, 1999)

Cc. Āśraya: A Diary While Attempting to Read Śrī Caitanya-caritāmṛta (1997)

From Copper to Touchstone: Favorite Selections from the Caitanya-caritāmṛta (1996)

Living With the Scriptures (1984)

My Search Through Books (1991)

Nīti-śāstras: Sayings of Cāṇakya and Hitopadeśa as Quoted by Śrīla Prabhupāda (1995)

Reading Reform Notebook (1985)

Readings in Vedic Literature (BBT 1977, reprinted as Elements of Vedic Thought and Culture)

The Qualities of Śrī Kṛṣṇa (1995)

Essay Collections

A Handbook for Kṛṣṇa Consciousness (1979)

Essays

Volume 1: A Handbook for Kṛṣṇa Consciousness: Back to Godhead 1966–1978 (2023)

Volume 2: From the Editor: Back to Godhead 1978–1989 (2023)

Volume 3: From the Road: Back to Godhead & Among Friends 1991–2004 (2023)

Spiritualized Dictionary (1997)

The Daily News: All Things Fail Without Kṛṣṇa (1994)

Radio Shows, Volumes 1, 2 (1995, 1997)

Poetry

108 Japa Poems 2010 (2010)

Can a White Man be a Haribol? (2003)

Daily Compositions (2020)

Gentle Power: Collected Poems 1995–1996 (1996)

Given Time: Poems (1999)

In Praise of the Mahājanas and Other Poems 1983 (1984)

Kaleidoscope (2020)

Meditations and Poems (2020)

Morning Songs (2011)

One Hundred Happy Ideas (1997)

Pictures from Bhagavad-gītā As It Is and Other Poems (1987)

Poems: A Retrospective, Volumes 1, 2 (2019)

Prose Poems at Castlegregory, Ireland (1994)

Rādhā-Govinda Reciprocate with Me (2023)

Songs from Stuyvesant Falls (2011)

Songs of a Hare Kṛṣṇa Man (1997)

Soul Eyes (2010)

Talking Freely to my Lords (1991)

The Dust of Vṛndāvana (1987, 2nd edition 2021)

The Voices of Surrender and Other Poems 1979–1982 (1982)

The Waves at Jagannātha Purī and Other Poems (1998)

The Worshipable Deity and Other Poems 1984 (1985)

Under the Banyan Tree (1986, 2nd edition 2021)

When the Saints Go Marching In: Poems by Satsvarūpa dāsa Goswami (2006)

Writing in Gratitude: Collected Poems 1992–1994 (1994)

Journals, Diaries, Travel Writings, Free Writing, Collected Writings

1996 Śrīla Prabhupāda Centennial Year Writings
Volume 1: May Apples (1996, 2nd edition 2024)
Volume 2: Basic Sketchbook (1996, 2nd edition 2024)
Volume 3: Upstate: Room to Write (1996, 2nd edition 2024)

Volume 4: June Bug (1996, 2nd edition 2024)
Volume 5: Geaglum Free Write Diary (1996, 2nd edition 2024)
Volume 6: Dublin Pieces (1996, 2nd edition 2024)
Volume 7: The Faithful Transcriber (1996, 2nd edition 2024)
Volume 8: Wicklow Writing Sessions (1996, 2nd edition 2024)
Volume9: Writing Sessions at Manu's House (1996, 2nd edition 2024)
Volume 10: My Purpose at Isola di Albarella (1996, 2nd edition 2024)

A Litany for The Gone (1996)

A Visit to Jagannātha Purī: A Pilgrimage Journal (1987)

Among Friends, Volumes 1–8 (1989–2004)

Ballyferriter Stories (1994)

Best Use of a Bad Bargain (2023)

Breaking the Silence: Selected Writings, 1991–1997 (1997)

Churning the Milk Ocean: Collected Writings, 1993–1994 (1996)

Every Day Just Write, Volumes 1–19 (1998-2003, Print), Volumes 20–76 (1998–2010, eBook)

Forgetting the Audience: Writing Sessions at Castlegregory, Ireland, 1993 (2021)

Human @t Best (2008)

I am Prabhupāda's Servant: September Catchall (1997)

ISKCON in the 1970s (1991)

Iṣṭa-Goṣṭhī: Topics for Vaiṣṇava Discussion, Volumes 1–3 (1989)

Journal and Poems, Volumes 1–3 (1985–1986)

Last Days of the Year (December 1994) (1998); (second edition 2021 as Last Days of the Year)

Lessons from the Road, Volumes 1–17 (1987–1988)

Passing Places, Eternal Truths: Travel Writings 1988–1996 (1998)

Progresso: A Ten-Day Book Seeking Kṛṣṇa Consciousness (1998)

Shack Notes: Moments While at a Writing Retreat (1992)

The Best I Could Do (2021)

The Journals of Satsvarūpa dāsa Goswami
Volume 0: Viraha Bhavan Journal, 2017–2018 (2018, 2024)
Volume 1: Worshiping with the Pen (2023)
Volume 2: Prabhupāda Revival (2023)
Volume 3: Be Prepared (2023)
Volume 4: Increasing the Presence of Prabhupāda (2023)
Volume 5: Renewal: Solving the Problem (2024)

The Wild Garden: Collected Writings From 1990–1993 (1994)

Fiction

Am I a Demon or a Vaiṣṇava? (1991)

Choṭa's Way (1990; 2nd edition 2023)

Gurudeva and Nimāi: Struggling for Survival (1989; 2nd edition 2023)

Nimāi Dāsa and the Mouse: A Fable (1989; 2nd edition 2023)

Nimāi's Detour: A Story (1989; 2nd edition 2023)

Pāda-yātrā (1998)

Sanatorium: A Novel (2005); new, revised edition (2023)

Seeking New Land: A Story (2020)

Śrī Caitanya Dayā: The Diaries of Harideva and Chāyadevī (1991)

The Nimāi Series: Single Volume Edition (2023)

Under Dark Stars: A Novel (2009)

Visitors (2007)

Viṣṇu-rāta Vijaya: The Story of an Ex-Hunter (1991)

Vraja-maṇḍala Lament: A Writer's Parikrama (2000)

Why Not Fiction? (1996)

Write & Die: A Novel (2006)

Art

Beginning at Second Avenue (n.d.)

From Matter to Spirit: Paintings, Poems, and Improvisations (2001)

Paintings and Sculpture (Exhibition Catalogue) (2001)

Photo Preaching (1996)

Sketchbooks of Joy (1997)

Splashes and Sacred Text: Collected Drawings and Paintings 1996–1997 (1998)

Stowies (2003)

The Many Colors of Satsvarūpa Dāsa Goswami (2017)

What's Going on Here? Kṛṣṇa Conscious Cartoons (2002)

Writing

In Search of the Grand Metaphor (1994; 2nd edition 2024)

Authored with Śrīla Prabhupāda

Mukunda-mālā-stotra: The Prayers of King Kulaśekhara (BBT 1992)

Nārada-bhakti-sūtra: The Secrets of Divine Love (BBT 1991)